The Soul Garden

The Soul Garden

DONALD NORFOLK

THE OVERLOOK PRESS
Woodstock & New York

First published in the United States in 2002 by
The Overlook Press, Peter Mayer Publishers, Inc.
Woodstock & New York

WOODSTOCK:
One Overlook Drive
Woodstock, NY 12498
www.overlookpress.com
[for individual orders, bulk and special sales, contact our Woodstock office]

NEW YORK:
141 Wooster Street
New York, NY 10012

Library of Congress Cataloging-in-Publication Data

Norfolk, Donald.
The soul garden : creating green spaces for inner growth
and spiritual renewal / Donald Norfolk.
p. cm.
includes bibliographical references.
1. Gardening—Religious aspects. 2. Gardens—Religious aspects.
3. Spiritual life. I. Title
BL629.5.G37 N67 2002 635'.01—dc21 2001053847

Manufactured in the United States of America
FIRST EDITION
1 3 5 7 9 8 6 4 2
ISBN 1-58567-236-X

To my green-fingered patients, who inspired me to write this book when I noted that their love of gardening seemed to imbue them with an above-average level of cheerfulness, contentment and physical fitness.

CONTENTS

*'And the Lord God planted a
garden eastward in Eden, and there
He put the man whom He
had formed.'*

GENESIS II, 8

GARDENS HAVE BEEN A TREASURED PART OF HUMAN culture for more than nine thousand years. From the Hanging Gardens of Babylon to the modest allotments of today's suburbia they have offered an oasis of civilization amid a maelstrom of violence, artifice and greed.

According to the folklore of the ancient Mediterranean people, mankind had its origin in a garden. Here our ancestors had their first encounter with God. Within the confines of this idyllic horticultural haven Adam and Eve led lives of joyous peace and plenty, and this ecstatic state might have persisted for ever had they not been exiled from bliss and forced to toil for their daily bread. Their fall from grace marked the entry into the world of evil, anguish and pain, and all our subsequent dreams of paradise have been shaped by the racial memory of this primordial Elysium. Deep down in the collective unconscious, the theory goes, there still lurks the belief that we could once again lead lives free of worry, strife and sickness if only we could recapture the carefree existence of that lost Garden of Eden.

This book examines this widespread belief, which was extolled by the nature poets and painters of the nineteenth century and promoted by philosophers such as Rousseau and Thoreau. It offers a simple way of harnessing the healing power of nature – the *vis medicatrix naturae* – through the cultivation of a garden plot, however modest in design and small in size. People *need* gardens today more than ever before. In an increasingly frenetic age they offer a vital source of comfort and an opportunity for mental, physical and spiritual renewal.

I invite you to join me in a journey of horticultural discovery, in the course of which you may find yourself undergoing a subtle change of character. For forty years, when I worked as an osteopath in the West End of London, I saw a remarkable cross-section of people from all walks of life: the great and the good, the rich and the poor, the famous and occasionally the blatantly infamous. The lifestyles of these people varied enormously and yet I noted that all those who were keen gardeners – whatever their social status – seemed to share certain behavioural characteristics. These men and women of the soil tended to be natural, 'down-to-earth' folk. By and large they were a contented bunch, with a spontaneous, phlegmatic approach to life. They were generally not health fanatics. They didn't pump iron, practise meditation or eat macrobiotic food, and yet they seemed to enjoy an above average level of physical and mental health. This book explores the secret of their well-being.

My aim is to provide a complete, step-by-step guide to the creation of a Soul Garden, providing practical hints on the way in which such a garden can be established and used to maximum effect.

Each of the twelve chapters in this book describes one of the essential principles of horticultural therapy. By following these steps, which might be described as the Twelve Axioms of Soul Gardening, you will be able to create your own holistic health sanctuary with whatever resources of time and space you have to hand.

Size is irrelevant, for even a window box or modest city courtyard or basement well can be developed to serve as an effective Soul Garden. If you live in the suburbs and are currently numbered among the horticulturally dispossessed, you could consider renting an allotment. In the city you might join a team of neighbours and set about the rewarding task of creating a Community Garden.

When we potter in a garden we take on something of the character of our natural surroundings. When we prune the roses, we automatically shed our aggression and harsh competitiveness and become more patient, peaceful and content.

While watering the hanging baskets, or tending a row of carrot seedlings, we develop the nurturative side of our psyches. When we create a beautiful herbaceous border we foster our artistic sense, balancing size, shape, colours and textures. During our working lives most of us use predominantly the left side of our brain, which deals with analytical thought, speech and logical reasoning. But when we garden we cultivate the right hemisphere, which is primarily concerned with aesthetic appreciation and intuitive thought. Most garden manuals offer a wide range of horticultural advice. They carry detailed technical instructions about plant propagation, soil acidity and grafting techniques, which exercise the left side of the brain. This book aims to stimulate the right hemisphere. It uses gardening not as an end in itself, but as an enjoyable means to a crucially important end, the promotion of wholeness, health and healing. Its prime concern is not to raise plants but to cultivate happier, healthier human beings.

The responsibility for the opinions expressed in this book lies with the author, but the credit for their appearance in this present form lies elsewhere. The concepts came from numerous sources; most notably from the writings of historians, philosophers, landscape gardeners, psychologists and medical researchers. Where possible their contribution has been acknowledged in the text, but many go unnamed and can only be credited here anonymously and en masse for their invaluable assistance.

It is fervently hoped that the publication of this book will act as a catalyst to stimulate interest in gardening as a therapeutic medium. To promote this development a website is being opened which will chronicle the latest advances in the field and offer a forum for world-wide interaction and debate. You are welcome to enter this dialogue and gain this ongoing encouragement and advice.

D. N.

The Soul Garden

INTRODUCTION: AN ANCIENT REMEDY

'Life must be lived forwards, but can only be understood backwards.'

SANTAYANA

THE ESTABLISHMENT OF HORTICULTURAL THERAPY AS A discrete scientific discipline is relatively new, but its roots are buried in antiquity, for gardening must surely be one of the oldest of all the healing arts. We live in a world of high technology, a rapidly evolving age of computers, jet planes, nuclear power and satellite global communication which would be totally alien to our great-grandparents. Yet the personal problems we suffer – unhappiness, sickness, loneliness, nervous anxiety, chronic fatigue and stress – are identical to theirs. While we are constantly seeking novel solutions to these common human predicaments, there is still a vast amount we can learn from the remedies of the past.

The human animal is a relatively recent arrival on the planet, having been in existence for little more than two million years. For the vast majority of this time *Homo sapiens* eked out a meagre living as a hunter gatherer. It is only in the last ten thousand years that our predecessors acquired the skills of agriculture which enabled them to give up their precarious nomadic lifestyle and establish permanent settlements. To compensate for this dramatic translocation, which tore them from their pastoral roots, they immediately began to create urban gardens to bring the countryside into the newly developing towns. While our forebears would be ill at ease with cars, television sets and mobile phones, they would recognize many of the plants in our gardens, for these have changed but marginally over the course of nine thousand years.

Archaeologists using carbon dating techniques have discovered that plants were first cultivated in the Jordan valley and along the eastern Black Sea coast before 7000 BC. The Hanging Gardens of Babylon, built out of a terraced hillside for the delight of King Nebuchadnezzar, were one of the earliest wonders of the ancient world. They gave shade in a land of searing heat and blistering sun. In the arid, semi-desert region of Babylonia, the Persian gardens offered a profusion of cooling pools and cascading water fountains. These gardens knew their purpose. They were designed primarily as spiritual retreats, as places of beauty, physical rest and mental repose. But what of the gardens which followed them?

During the Roman Empire gardens were created to provide pleasure grounds for their aristocratic owners. They were established on the outskirts of the rapidly growing Mediterranean cities, largely as an escape from the rush and bustle of metropolitan life. The wealthy inhabitants of Jerusalem maintained gardens on the slopes of the Mount of Olives. It was to one of these that Jesus took his disciples whenever he felt the need to escape the crowds and find a measure of rest and peace.

In medieval times gardens served a more utilitarian function. Monasteries and grand manorial homes needed to be self-sufficient, so their grounds were filled with orchards, vegetable gardens, dovecotes, pigsties, chicken runs, herbariums and stew ponds stocked with fish. With the coming of the agricultural revolution there was less need for self-sufficiency gardening, since fruit and vegetables could be grown more economically on large-scale commercial farms. It was then that wealthy landowners found an alternative use for their gardens – as status symbols. This was the era of the grand seventeenth-century Franco-Italian gardens, with their strictly regimented borders, parterres, paths, ponds and fountains. These were so expensive to construct, and so costly to maintain, that they provided a conspicuous demonstration of their owners' wealth. Who but a king like Louis XIV could afford to build a garden with the vastness of scale and architectural magnificence of Versailles?

The English landscape gardens of the eighteenth century came as a welcome reaction to the excesses of Franco-Italian formalism. These gardens were created by artists such as William Kent and 'Capability' Brown, who were inspired by the Romantic movement which was sweeping Europe with the whirlwind force of a spiritual revival. Gardens were now designed chiefly for their aesthetic impact, and like a Corot landscape painting they became areas of romance, mystery and beauty, filled with foliage, ponds, classical statues, grottoes, out-door pavilions, ruined temples and meandering paths.

A generation later romance gave way to science. Gardens

ceased to be places of wild, natural beauty and were transformed into horticultural laboratories. Imperialist explorers were travelling the world and bringing back hordes of exotic plants, which it was fashionable to acquire and display. A Scottish collector visited Chile and smuggled back a single cone from a monkey-puzzle tree. From this one fruit he produced five plants and from these many, many more. Within a few years gardeners from Penzance to Perth were fighting to display the remarkable monkey-puzzle tree, and gained extra kudos if they could refer to it by its official Latin name, *Araucaria araucana*. This was the age of the plantsman's garden, when there was a premium on rare and exotic flora. Plants were collected and displayed like postage stamps. At this time it was often more important to know a flower's Latin name than to appreciate its delicious scent or beautiful colouring. Plants lost their descriptive folk names; Stinking Nanny became known as *Senecio Jacobaea*, and the lively 'Jack-jump-up-and-kiss-me' was transformed into the prosaic *Viola tricolor*.

The horticultural elite today may still maintain gardens which are largely botanical showcases. Other gardeners have no great interest in the biological sciences. For them gardening is merely a healthy outdoor pursuit, an alternative perhaps to going for a drive in the country or visiting a shopping centre. This trend can be traced back to the development of the suburbs, which provided allotments and back gardens where white-collar workers could while away their precious leisure hours free from the suffocating pall of city smoke. On these treasured patches of private land they could indulge their fancy for growing prize dahlias, propagating gladioli or cultivating a weed-free lawn.

No two gardens are alike or ever have been. They are subject to fashion trends, just like pop music and haute couture. They are also conditioned by the vagaries of the particular garden plot: its size, setting, topographical features, drainage and soil characteristics. But more especially they are dependent on the taste, personality and lifestyle of their owners. In this way form follows function. Millions of people around the world maintain gardens, but the chances are that very, very few have ever sat down and considered the functions their garden serves. The land may be used as a playground for children or a place to hang out the washing, to grow vegetables, to house bicycle sheds, to tip waste, to exercise the dog, to hold barbecues or simply to laze on sunny days.

What is the prime attraction of gardening for *you*? That was the question asked recently of a large group of British gardeners. Most of their answers pointed in some way to the therapeutic benefits of gardening. Some said they welcomed the opportunity to be in the open air, to enjoy physical exercise, to satisfy their creative urge and to have contact with living plants. Others extolled the pleasure of having an absorbing hobby and the independence they gained from growing their own fruit and vegetables.

THE CANDIDE SOLUTION

THROUGHOUT THE COURSE OF ITS HISTORY THERE HAVE BEEN constant references to the health-giving effects of gardening, most of them purely anecdotal and unsupported by medical research. Robert Burton, in his scholarly seventeenth-century study *The Anatomy of Melancholy*, claimed that one of the finest cures for despondency was to take a gentle walk around a garden. This was a theme frequently taken up by novelists in later years. Voltaire told the story of Candide, who, after enduring many tribulations in his search for wisdom and serenity, eventually found true contentment through cultivating a garden. It was here, rather than in some distant hall of spiritual enlightenment, that Candide discovered the tranquillity he sought and arrived at the reassuring conclusion that 'All is for the best in the best of possible worlds.'

The therapeutic powers of gardening were also highlighted in *The Secret Garden*, the highly successful Edwardian children's book by Frances Hodgson Burnett. The romance relates how a spoilt orphan girl called Mary Lennox travels to the Yorkshire Dales to live with her uncle. In the grounds of his house she discovers a neglected walled garden, hidden behind a locked gate. She starts to tend the garden and discovers that its natural beauty has the power to cure her uncle's grief, the longstanding illness of her cousin Colin and her own unhappiness. There is a telling moment in the story when Colin is taken from his sickbed into the garden and is overwhelmed by the sight of the grass and the trees, the scent of the flowers, the humming of the bees and the gentle warmth of the sun playing on his face. The experience unleashes in him the healing powers of nature and gives him back the will to recover. 'I shall get well, I shall get well!' he cries out to Mary. 'And I shall live for ever and ever and ever!'

Many eminent people have paid similar witness to the curative power of gardening. Here, for instance, is the testimony of Ralph Waldo Emerson, written in 1853: 'When I go into my garden, and dig a bed, I feel such an exhilaration and health that

I discover that I have been defrauding myself all this time in letting others do for me what I should have done with my own hands.'

THE BIRTH OF
HORTICULTURAL THERAPY

IN VIEW OF THESE REPEATED TRIBUTES AND PERSONAL CASE histories it seems remarkable that the medical profession was so slow to harness the healing power of gardening. It began to be adopted as a therapy in the eighteenth and nineteenth centuries, when mental asylums were equipped with gardens so that inmates could escape the boredom of close confinement and take a few hours' healthy outdoor exercise. Benjamin Rush, writing in 1798, noted that gardening had 'a curative effect' on mentally ill patients held in American asylums. This belief was shared by many other specialists in mental health care. In 1856 the rules of the Dorset County Asylum, for example, stipulated that male patients should be employed as much as possible in the garden 'to promote cheerfulness and happiness among them'.

Nowadays we try to achieve these ends with psychotropic drugs, but such medicines are not necessarily curative and can lead to drug dependency and a wide range of untoward side effects. As a result some doctors are once again recommending horticultural therapy for patients with mental health problems, especially when they are living in the community rather than in enclosed institutions. In Nottingham, the Worksop District Council has provided allotments for patients suffering from conditions such as schizophrenia, anxiety and depression. These patients are now encouraged to don their Wellington boots and grow Brussels sprouts, onions and potatoes. 'If it wasn't for this place, we'd be at home or at a day centre, or just walking around town,' said one allotment holder.

Other doctors are making use of garden therapy in the rehabilitation of the physically disabled and geriatrically handicapped. It is also being used to speed the recovery of post-operative patients. Research has revealed that hospital patients recover more quickly from surgical operations when they are given the chance to feast their eyes on grass and trees. As the *British Medical Journal* has stated, 'Recent research in environmental psychology is now giving encouragement to the call for the revival of the old tradition of providing gardens for hospital patients,' along the lines of the convalescent courtyards attached to medieval hospices.

But gardening is far more than occupational therapy for the disabled and sick: it is a life-expanding experience for all. In a garden we can find a cure for boredom and chronic fatigue; a remedy for unhappiness, and an escape from feelings of tension, anxiety, alienation and futility. If prevention is better than cure, why is the application of horticultural therapy being restricted to the treatment of the sick, when it could be employed for the health promotion of every man, woman and child?

Boredom is one of the major debilitating diseases of our age, especially for people who are forced to carry out routine tasks in enclosed work spaces. For some time Russian scientists experimented to discover how they could keep their astronauts cheerful and fit while in orbit around the earth for months on end in a tiny spacecraft. One suggestion was to give them a chance to garden during their flights. To test this theory, a steel chamber was built to resemble a spaceship in size and shape. Inside was a miniature garden, equipped with small 'allotment' trays on which plants and vegetables could be grown. Two men then took their place in the cabin, where they were incarcerated for spells of fifteen to forty days. Observations showed that nearly half the steps they took inside the chamber led them to the garden, either to tend the plants or just for the primeval pleasure of watching things grow. Tiny though their plot was, it still played a major role in maintaining their well-being.

A UTOPIAN ENVIRONMENT

MOST OF OUR CONCEPTS OF CELESTIAL HEAVENS AND EARTHLY utopias are firmly placed in a garden setting. However materialistic our outlook, we don't expect to find heaven in a supermarket or nightclub. In fact the word 'paradise' is derived from the Persian for 'walled garden'. This is the longed-for destination of all devout Muslims, who are assured in the Koran: 'Allah has promised the men and women who believe in Him gardens watered by running streams, in which they shall abide for ever.' This dream of heaven has been shared by poets, philosophers and social reformers for countless years.

One of the first written accounts of paradise was provided by Homer, who gave this description of Olympus, the mountain playground of the gods: 'Outside the courtyard, near the door is a large four-acre orchard, with a fence on either side. Here trees grow tall in rich profusion, pears, pomegranates, glowing apples, luscious figs, olives in profusion.' Amaurote, the capital city of Sir Thomas More's cluster of paradise islands, was similarly conceived. It was bisected by a tidal river and surrounded by a twenty-four-mile band of green. Before people could take up residence in the city, they had to serve a two-year apprenticeship in the countryside, so they would learn agricultural skills and come to appreciate the beauty of nature. Every house in Amaurote had its own garden, which the owners maintained with enormous pride. As More relates in *Utopia*, the people's passion for gardening 'is increased not merely by the pleasure afforded them, but by the keen competition between streets, which shall have the best kept garden'. Even the infamous Casanova, who placed his fantasy paradise underground, still contrived to have it filled with glorious gardens which somehow managed to flourish even though they were far removed from the nourishment of sun and rain.

Years later town planners set out to give substance to these pastoral dreams. Ebenezer Howard founded the city of Welwyn amid rural land in Hertfordshire. The city was filled with public parks and private gardens, and surrounded by a green belt of trees and fields. This cordon sanitaire kept the inhabitants in close touch with nature and also put a strict check on urban sprawl. Architects wanted to call these utopian communities 'green-belt towns', but the public thought otherwise and by popular demand they became known as 'garden cities'. Howard himself wrote a book called *Garden Cities of Tomorrow*. The hygienists of the day gave their full support, for they firmly believed that parks and gardens served an essential sanitary function, providing the 'lungs' of cities which were becoming increasingly crowded and polluted.

SIMPLE PLEASURES

TODAY, EVEN IF WE ARE SUPER RICH, WE MAY NOT THINK IT APPRO-priate to flaunt our wealth by constructing conspicuous status symbols like the gardens of the Alhambra or Versailles. Perhaps we have no time for hobby gardening, and little need of a utilitarian garden now that we have supermarkets offering a vast array of cheap, fresh fruits and vegetables. But these developments have not rendered gardening obsolete. In fact gardens are more vital now than ever before. The days of the botanical garden may be coming to an end, but the era of the Soul Garden has only just begun. As we confront the revolutionary changes which the new millennium is bound to bring, we will have greater need for private gardens which offer a brief respite from the artificiality, bustle, transience and ugliness of our daily lives. In a pressurized world where today is too early and tomorrow too late, we will need to retreat into our private havens and rediscover the joys of simplicity.

One way to achieve contentment is to reduce our needs to the point where they can be satisfied by a less sophisticated way of life. Alice Bay Laurel, author of *Living on the Earth*, gives this sure recipe for relaxation and repose: 'Find a little bit of land somewhere and plant a carrot seed. Now sit down and watch it grow. When it is fully grown pull it up and eat it.' Anyone who can adopt that simple philosophy is unlikely to have need of tranquillizers or sleeping pills.

WHOSE CONCERN?

MANY PEOPLE TODAY ARE CONCERNED ABOUT ENVIRONMENTAL issues. Quite rightly they worry about the pollution of the atmosphere, the despoliation of the countryside, the loss of native birds and flowers and the insidious spread of towns and motorways. We look for scapegoats, but in the last analysis all our social ills are self-inflicted. Ecological problems have arisen because we ourselves have made inappropriate choices.

Urban growth in Britain has been paving over an area the size of Bristol every year. In the midst of this concrete desert we must make sure that gardens flourish and parks flower. If in future we spend more of our leisure time in our own gardens we will have less call for new motorways and fewer traffic jams. When we patronize theme parks, amusement arcades, gymnasiums and sports centres we treat entertainment and exercise as bolt-on extras rather than as integral parts of a full and rounded life. The Soul Garden of the future will fulfil all these needs under one, sky-clad roof.

The chapters which follow provide the rules for creating such a garden, which are mainly derived from the great and ancient tradition of garden design. The Soul Garden serves in part as a pleasure garden, as it did in the days of King Nebuchadnezzar. It brings us into close touch with nature, as did the great British landscape gardens of the early nineteenth century. It incorporates some of the features of the utilitarian gardens of the medieval monasteries, and some of the attributes of the hobby gardens of more recent times. But at this point it would be wise to insert a government health warning. We are dealing here with an exceedingly powerful remedy, and although gardening has no serious side effects (apart from splinters, broken nails and aching backs) it can be *very* addictive.

CHAPTER ONE

Back to Nature

'A garden is not merely a piece of nature
fenced in near the house, like a
wolf chained at the back door; but
nature cultivated and trained like
a dog tamed and trained for
human ends.'

ABRAM LINWOOD URBAN

*T*HIRTY-FIVE YEARS AGO I WAS ASKED TO REVIEW A BOOK called *Man Adapting* by René Dubos, a world-famous bacteriologist who was then Emeritus Professor of Environmental Biomedicine at Rockefeller University, New York. The book contained a simple yet profound message: that man is essentially a pastoral animal poorly equipped to cope with a modern urban existence. As Dubos wrote: 'Life in the modern city has become a symbol of the fact that man can become adapted to starless skies, treeless avenues, shapeless buildings, tasteless bread, joyless celebration, spiritless pleasures.' Those words have echoed in my mind ever since.

We are in many respects too adaptable for our own good. We can survive in our concrete jungles, even fool ourselves that we are enjoying the amusements and material comforts they provide, and yet deep down we know that something is seriously lacking. We miss our contact with the natural world. To compensate for this loss we watch wildlife films on television, furnish our city apartments with indoor plants and decorate our offices with tanks of tropical fish. If we are wealthy, we may buy a second home in the country and at weekends try to lead lives of rural self-sufficiency. Today's growth sports – country walking, sailing, rock climbing, camping, skiing, horse riding and whitewater rafting – are all designed to take us into the great outdoors. Stressed executives go fishing, not primarily to catch fish, most of which are inedible and are tossed back into the water, but to spend a few hours in close and quiet communion with nature.

At the weekends city workers jump into their cars and join the bumper-to-bumper cavalcades to visit the countryside.

Many take their children to zoos and wildlife parks. A recent survey revealed that more adults and children visit zoos in America than attend all the major professional sporting events combined. Menageries are equally popular in Europe, so much so that at one time Zurich Zoo was having far more visitors each year than the city had inhabitants. We feel a need to escape our urban environments and recapture our links with the birds and beasts of the field – but would it not be more satisfying to establish a closer rapport with the sparrows and robins in our garden than to make occasional sorties to watch the displays of peacocks penned in artificial surroundings?

Office workers in Japan find alternative ways of satisfying their pastoral longings. They form groups to hold moon-watching parties, or to visit the cherry orchards in the spring to marvel at the beauty of the newly opening blossom. In the summer and autumn they tour the farms to pick strawberries, apples, mandarins and grapes, or go into the fields to dig peanuts and sweet potatoes. But like us they also prize their gardens, which provide a popular leisure pursuit for over 32 million Japanese, nearly a third of the country's population.

People who live in cramped conditions feel a particular need for contact with nature. When a group of astronauts of various nationalities was asked to provide suggestions for the interior decoration of their capsules, they were unanimous in their desire for more indoor plants and landscape paintings. As one investigator observed: 'Human beings' love for nature and natural materials and forms, especially in high technology habitats, seems to transcend national boundaries.' This is confirmed by trials which reveal that office workers show a strong preference for windows with views over natural, outdoor scenery. When this outlook is denied them, they are more likely to hang landscape paintings on their walls than workers who have the benefit of an outdoor view.

Experiments have shown that people are not only happier when they maintain some contact with the world of nature, but also demonstrably healthier. Prisoners whose cells look out on forests and open farmland suffer fewer spells of sickness than those whose view is restricted to buildings and prison walls. In another study people were artificially stressed and then monitored as they watched video films during a ten-minute recovery period. Some watched films which showed everyday street scenes, while others relaxed by watching a video of natural scenery rich in vegetation. The responses of the two groups differed to a significant degree: the people viewing the pastoral scenes showed faster falls in anger, anxiety, pulse rate, muscle tension and blood pressure.

As a race we have inhabited planet earth for at least two million years. For 99 per cent of this time we led a nomadic existence. It is only in the last ten thousand years that we have mastered the art of farming and learned to live in towns. This is a mere blink in the annals of recorded time. Deep down we still feel displaced, and yearn to regain contact with our pastoral roots. In the past the importance of this link was largely ignored by the medical profession. Scientists were so preoccupied with the *adverse* effects of environmental factors – polluted water supplies, mineral-deficient soils, acid rain and airborne germs and parasites – that they failed to recognize the *beneficial* effects that human beings derive from close communion with their natural milieu. This blinkered view is changing fast. Numerous studies have shown that patients are profoundly affected by their contact with the natural world. Some people keep pets because they satisfy the fundamental human need to love and be loved. Many gardeners derive a similar satisfaction when they tend their flower beds and vegetable gardens. Arthur Miller, the American playwright, couldn't understand why he spent so much time and effort raising carrots and beetroots, vegetables he didn't particularly enjoy and could always buy at the local supermarket. Then he realized that gardening was for him not so much a subsistence exercise as a form of moral and occupational therapy. 'Whenever life seems pointless and difficult to grasp,' he wrote, 'you can always get out in the garden and get *something done*. Also, your paternal or maternal instincts come into play, because helpless living things are depending on you, require training and encouragement and protection from enemies.'

This inter-species caring and sharing affects the way we feel and how we behave. A survey of over five thousand patients attending a heart disease risk clinic at the Baker Medical Research Institute in Prahan, Australia, revealed that the blood pressure and blood cholesterol levels of pet owners are significantly lower than in people who do not have an animal mate. The overall effect of these changes is estimated to bring about a 4 per cent reduction in the risk of heart attacks.

ROOTED IN NATURE

HOWEVER HARD WE TRY, WE CAN NEITHER CONTROL THE FORCES OF nature nor divorce ourselves from their effect. Medicine is at last accepting the reality of this fact. Dogs and cats are being prescribed like pills, especially for sick children and lonely geriatric patients, who are thought to be the main beneficiaries of what is now classified as Pet Facilitated Therapy. Psychologists have launched a new discipline – ecopsychology – to explore our interrelationship with animals, plants, trees, rivers and rocks. These studies may seem far removed from our daily lives and yet they throw light on many of our contemporary problems. We cannot ignore our links with nature. These ties are not a matter of choice. Whether we like it or not, we are an inextricable part of our natural environment. This is an issue we must confront, if only because it influences our long-term well-being. In a 1982 statement called the *World Charter of Nature*, a United Nations commission concluded: 'Civilisation is rooted in nature, which has shaped human culture and influenced all artistic and scientific achievement, and living in harmony with nature gives man the best opportunities for the development of his creativity, and for rest and recreation.'

Gardening provides one simple way of maintaining our atavistic pastoral roots and thereby making the most of our opportunities for creativity, rest and recreation. When we construct a garden, we surround ourselves with a green cocoon which serves as a microcosm of the natural world. In order to maintain his contact with the earth, in the sixth century AD the Chinese emperor Yang Ti ordered the creation around his palace of a lake-filled park more than sixty miles in circumference. Many of his subjects followed his example. Being far too poor to build gardens on the imperial scale, they perfected the art of miniaturization. For them a single, water-washed rock became the symbol of a mighty crag. A tiny pond created the image of a giant lake, and two sentinel trees became the metaphor for a towering forest. With their love of myth, the Chinese used the symbol of a bridge thrown across a miniature pond to suggest the fantasy Isle of the Immortals, a utopian sanctuary which was said to lie somewhere in the Eastern Ocean. These images were incorporated in their traditional pottery designs, which often include the figure of a misshapen man. He is one of the world's earliest named gardeners, a man known as the Ugly Artisan, who worked to create the gardens of the Imperial Palace of Japan in AD 612.

THE NOBLE SAVAGE

DURING PERIODS OF RAPID SOCIAL UPHEAVAL OR TECHNOLOGICAL change, there is often a longing to return to the 'good old days' of rural simplicity. Tacitus, the Roman historian, looked with envy at the vigorous, unsophisticated lifestyles of the barbarian people living in the Rhineland forests in the first century AD. He believed that they retained their primeval purity, courage and high moral standards because they had not been corrupted by Roman materialism and greed. Their children might grow up naked and dirty, but they were lusty and strong. In developing this simplistic argument in his *Germania* he invented the myth of the Noble Savage.

A similar feeling surfaced in Europe towards the end of the nineteenth century. At the century's start people were enjoying the benefits of the Industrial Revolution and had every confidence that the new technology would usher in a world of affluence, comfort and ease. By the time it drew to a close the ebullient mood had changed, and people were fearful that industrialization had created a technological hell awash with violence, crime, smog, squalor and urban overcrowding. Social reformers such as William Morris urged an escape from materialism and a return to a culture which valued beauty, freedom and natural simplicity above crass monetary gain. People responded to the call of the Romantic poets, who diagnosed the fundamental malaise of Victorian life as a schism between thinking and feeling. The chief ills, which Matthew Arnold identified in his poem 'Dover Beach', were a lack of time, a dearth of beauty in the artificial, man-made world and an alienation from the world of nature.

Those same ills are with us today. Our technological cleverness has isolated us from the world of nature and we yearn to return to the simplicity of the Garden of Eden, especially when we are bombarded by media reports reminding us of the man-made dangers of global warming, soil erosion, poisoned food chains, collapsing fisheries, falling water tables, shrinking forests and dying lakes.

THE SIGHING OF THE WIND

WE LONG TO ESCAPE, BUT WE CANNOT LIVE FOR EVER IN A WORLD of dreams. Arcadia never existed, and utopia will never ensue. Our environmental problems are with us in the here and now and demand immediate solution. It is only in relatively recent years that we have gained sufficient power to make significant impact on the natural order of events. Many people are fearful that our environmental tinkering will pose a threat to the human race but, while it would be foolish to ignore the long-term risks, I feel sure that we will escape an ecological Armageddon once we have had time to adapt to the changes we have made. This biological adjustment may take many generations to come into effect. During this time our welfare may be at risk. In 1976 Professor John Pemberton, delivering the Milroy Lecture to the Royal College of Physicians in London, spoke of the need to study the health implications of the close link between human beings and their environment: 'If it is accepted that most diseases are the result of a disturbance of the "equilibrium between man and surrounding nature" it follows that research that includes the environmental component is more likely to be successful in uncovering the etiology of disease and in devising methods of control than research directed to man alone or the environment alone.'

So the hunt is on to find causal links between environmental influences and human malaise. In the 1990s Japanese officials became troubled by the costly impact of stress upon their fellow citizens. To investigate the problem, they convened a study group of civil servants, scientists, sociologists and university professors. Eventually the panel concluded that the finest way to combat stress was to return to the traditional pastimes of dwarf tree cultivation (bonsai), flower arranging (ikebana) and simply 'listening to the sigh of the wind in the trees'.

The dramatic change from peasant farming to office work has imposed severe strains on our powers of physiological adaptation. The modern city is a stressful place in which to live and work. At times we find the noise and hectic pace intolerable. Some complain about the oppressive overcrowding – and yet modern town dwellers are far less densely packed today than, for example, their Cro-Magnon forebears in the south of France who were often confined two hundred or more in a single cave. We suffer anxiety when we get caught up in the rat race, over-loaded with work and plagued with tight deadlines, job insecurity and excessive competition. But how can this distress be compared with the terror our ancestors experienced when they left the safety of their caves and came face to face with a woolly rhinoceros? Stress is not new, it is an inescapable part of human experience. What has changed is the *nature* of the stress. In the course of our lives today we rarely get a chance to escape from the incessant pressure, bustle and din. This provokes a biological response which has not changed since our species evolved. Our muscles tense, our pulse races, our blood pressure soars and our bloodstreams are flooded with extra glucose and fat to prepare us for vigorous muscular activity. This is an atavistic defence mechanism which prepares us for 'fight or flight'. But whereas the cave dwellers' stress was quickly over – either they were killed by the rhinoceros or they escaped to the safety of their cave – ours can go on undiminished for weeks or months on end. So we become the victims of stress-related ill-ness, ranging from relatively benign tension headaches and muscular rheumatism to potentially fatal hypertension and coronary disease.

We desperately need a foxhole into which we can escape. Soldiers suffer breakdowns in health if they are kept for too long in the front line, which is why they are given regular spells of rest and recreation well away from the action zone. We too need our breaks for R & R if we are to avoid the consequences of battle fatigue. These recovery spells need not be long but they should be frequent, and are best spent in a peaceful, natural setting. At one time the countryside was at everyone's back door, whereas now we have to travel miles on crowded motorways to reach a patch of unpolluted countryside. As a compensation some people today listen to CDs which promise to soothe away the stresses of everyday life with recordings of the natural sounds of tropical rainforests and Caribbean sea shores, and the haunting, submarine calls of Pacific whales. But there is no need to look so far afield, for the same effect can be obtained by sitting quietly in a garden listening to the mellifluous notes of blackbirds and thrushes.

THE PRIME CULPRIT

THE ENVIRONMENTAL PROBLEMS WE FACE TODAY ARE MAINLY OF our own making. *We* are polluting the environment, *we* are filling our cities with unwanted noise, *we* are creating traffic jams, *we* are the ones who are replacing green-field sites with housing estates, shopping malls and factories. In the past there has always been a balance in nature between predator and prey. Now that balance has been shattered. One creature – by sheer technological genius – has achieved supremacy over the rest of the biosphere. We are seeking to control, rather than to live in harmony with, our natural environment. We have outlawed tribal warfare, human sacrifice and cannibalism. Antibiotics have largely eliminated our bacterial predators, which has greatly reduced the incidence of tuberculosis, syphilis and typhoid fever. As a result we are multiplying rapidly and destroying the rest of the natural world. Like Faust, we have sold our immortal souls for short-term material gain.

At present we are looking to governments to find an escape from the ecological wasteland we have created. But people in authority, whether they are business tycoons, politicians or military leaders, have gained their ascendance by harnessing the power of technology and mass communication. If we are to lessen our dependence on machines and achieve a closer relationship with nature, we cannot expect to gain support from the ruling elite, for they have a vested interest in maintaining the status quo. Nor will help come from the mass media, which attract public attention by stressing problems rather than advancing practical solutions. If change is to come it will have to come from below – from the ground up. It will, in fact, have to be a truly grass-roots movement.

The desire to rediscover our grass roots is strong. According to a 1991 Gallup poll, seven out of ten Britons have no doubt that the quality of life is greater in the country than in the town. However, it is important to remember that while many people become disenchanted with their everyday lives and harbour dreams of giving up their jobs and sailing round the world, the reality of moving out can be a painful experience. For example, Paul Gauguin, a successful French stockbroker, became the envy of Europe when he abandoned his career and escaped to Tahiti to paint and enjoy a beachcomber's life of idleness and pleasure. It sounded idyllic, but the truth was very different. Gauguin earned so little money as an artist that he was forced to work as a labourer, mending the island roads for six francs a day. He died disillusioned, penniless and bitter at the age of fifty-five. He would have been better advised to keep his day job at the Bourse and escape to a wilderness garden during the evenings and at weekends. That was the compromise made by Lewis

Mumford, the world-famous authority on town development. He recognized the need that most city dwellers have to retain their links with the natural world. Throughout his life he lived and worked in New York but he was a keen gardener, and for over forty years he maintained a rural bolt-hole in Dutchess County. He had no complaints about city life but confessed: 'I do need solitude every day, and some contact with nature in a more or less primitive form.'

The more time we spend in natural surroundings, the more we acquire the attributes of nature. Our lives take on the qualities of our environment, becoming more ordered, stable and harmonious. We need to work, but we also need to find time to escape from the marketplace. It's useful to have money and the things that money can buy, but it's equally important to make sure that we don't lose the things which money cannot buy, such as beauty, peace of mind and time for reflection. These gifts are freely available within a Soul Garden.

When we are enjoying the simple pleasures of gardening we soon learn the crucial lesson that contentment stems, not from having all we want, but from simply having enough.

We need to fight the ecological war on two fronts. At present we are waging a purely rearguard action, trying to stop the steady encroachment of the city into green-field sites. Instead, we should be waging a more subtle war of infiltration. As our towns and cities spread outwards, we should be moving in and creating pastoral enclaves within the deprived inner cities. It's not enough to surround our towns with green belts; we must, whenever possible, create green belts around our individual homes. This is the first function of the Soul Garden, to enable us to overcome our alienation from the world of nature so that we become active nature *livers* rather than abstract nature *lovers*.

THE ACADEMY OF NATURE

GARDENS CAN BE SANCTUARIES OF THE SOUL, IF THEY BRING US BACK into contact with the earth. When we are fully grounded we become aware of the values which shape our lives. For one thing, we discover how very little we require to satisfy our basic needs. Somewhere during the course of human development we have developed a craving to acquire far more than we need to support our day-to-day existence. We have become like budgerigars, living in beautifully gilded cages equipped with mirrors, toys, exercise wheels and regularly replenished food troughs. We have never been so well endowed nor at the same time – in Macbeth's words – so 'cabined, cribbed, confined'.

In the garden we can escape the artificiality of our daily lives and the social conventions that go with it. Within our own wild spaces we are no longer on public display. We can dress as we please and act as oddly as we choose – indeed, many long-term gardeners display a delightful eccentricity of style.

Within this environment our doomsday fears of impending ecological disasters are lessened as we learn to trust the restorative power of the natural order. Anyone who has watched the weeds breaking through a concrete path will have no doubt that the generative force of nature will always triumph over man's puny powers of self-destruction. Many of our environmental worries arise because we grossly exaggerate our technological prowess. Once we prayed for rain and held fertility dances to increase the productivity of the land. Now we seed the clouds with ice and spread the land with chemical fertilizers, thinking that we are masters of all we survey. But gardeners know otherwise. They know that the most serious mistake you can make in a garden is to think that you're in charge!

Sitting in a wilderness garden you can almost hear the generative power of nature. It is like watching a speeded-up film, when buds uncurl, flowers open and shrubs expand as if by magic. If we were to leave a patch of land free from human intervention – no cropping, mowing, digging or ploughing – it would quickly revert to its natural state. If left uncultivated, within a few years the entire surface of England would be covered by a wild woodland of sycamore, ash, silver birch, hawthorns, brambles, elderberries and wild roses. It is this feeling of wild, unfettered energy one seeks to create in a Soul Garden. The trick is to plant and then stand back and let the garden grow by a process of natural succession. After that it is only necessary to shape and prune, using the most delicate touch to create the impression that the garden has appeared of its own accord, with no human intervention.

PRETTY AS A PICTURE

NOWADAYS WE MEASURE TIME IN NANOSECONDS, WHICH MAKES IT difficult for us to grasp the concepts of eternity and timelessness. We feel comfortable when distances are measured in millimetres, but are bewildered by notions of infinity and limitless cosmic space. At work we have become increasingly tiny cogs in an ever-expanding wheel; work is divorced from play and also from family and community life. Indeed, our social lives are divided. During the day we play a variety of different roles – parent, lover, neighbour, teacher, colleague, social activist, amateur musician, collector of antique scent bottles. Everything is piecemeal and chaotic, with our lives pervaded by a constant sense of restlessness and disarray. This problem was highlighted over a century ago by the psychologist William James, who suggested that a high proportion of our contemporary angst was caused by 'the fragmentation of our lives'. The German word he chose to describe this troublesome new malaise, *Zerrissenheit*, means 'torn-to-pieces-hood'.

One aim of the Soul Garden is to restore a feeling of integrity. The landscape gardens of eighteenth-century Britain were called 'picturesque' because they resembled pictures. Whatever their size, they were not random collections of vegetable beds, orchards, herb gardens, potting sheds and greenhouses but balanced compositions, like the paintings of the great French landscape artists Watteau, Boucher and Fragonard. Formal gardens have the contrapuntal exactness of a Bach concerto, whereas a Soul Garden should convey the soaring freedom and lyricism of a Beethoven sonata. The ideal is to create an integrated landscape painting, so that the eye is captured by the overall picture rather than drawn to individual features. Within this holistic setting we are made aware, not of the cleverness of the gardener, but of the *megalophyia* or 'greatness of Nature'. Within this environment we are enabled to escape the *Zerrissenheit* of our daily lives and feel at one with the cosmic whole, a metaphysical experience which we must now explore in greater depth.

nature

Whatever its size, the Soul Garden should be designed to create a miniature nature reserve, a space where birds nest and foliage grows luxuriant. This is our ancestral habitat, for we are by nature and nurture a pastoral people. Our forebears lived in close contact with the land. Their lives were hard, but natural, ordered and free. Ours, by contrast, are artificial and chaotic. Our ears are assailed, not by the gentle call of the birds, but by the constant cacophony of traffic and mobile phones. Our eyes are no longer soothed by the delicate fluttering of the leaves, but bedazzled by the flickering of computer monitors and TV screens.

As yet we have not had time to adapt to life in our technological mazes and as a result we suffer psychosocial distress, which is revealed in statistics showing that rates of crime, divorce, mental breakdown and suicide are consistently higher in towns than in the country. To avoid this stress we need to go back occasionally to a simpler, pastoral way of life. And where better to do this than in a garden, where we can escape the pressures of our working lives and enjoy a brief return to the solace, spontaneity and freedom of nature.

To achieve this effect a Soul Garden should be irregular, wild and unrestrained; a place where the artificialities of modern life are left behind and where we are made acutely conscious of the power of nature to grow, sustain and heal.

CHAPTER TWO

Mother Earth

'It is a very comfortable thing to
stand in your own ground,
Land is about the only thing
that can't fly away.'

ANTHONY TROLLOPE

*W*E ARE CREATURES OF THE EARTH. THIS IS OUR natural habitat, the place where we feel most at home and most secure. We may be perched for part of our lives in high-rise office blocks, but we are generally more at ease when we come down to ground level. Like Antaeus in the Greek myth, we derive our potency from our contact with mother earth. Antaeus, the son of the earth goddess, became a champion wrestler because he gained fresh strength whenever he was thrown to the ground. He was finally defeated by Hercules who, knowing his secret, held him up in the air so that he was far removed from the source of his vitality and power. We suffer a similar enervation when we lose contact with the soil, for it is the substrate from which all human life springs and to which all human life eventually returns.

Human cultures acknowledge many different creation myths, most of which share a common belief that men and women were originally formed from the earth. Adam gained his name because he was born of the earth (from the Hebrew *adama*). His duty, according to the Old Testament, was not to tame the wilderness but to 'serve the earth'. The Babylonians shared a similar tradition, believing that man was made from a mixture of dust and the blood of one of the lesser gods. As a result they drew no sharp distinction between men and the gods, because both were thought to stem from the one common substance. The Apache Indian view of creation was slightly different. They believed that man was born from deep inside the womb of mother earth. The earth was their mother lying face upwards to the sky, and their father was the downward-facing sky. The rain which fertilized the land was the downpouring of his celestial semen.

The lives of primitive people were inextricably linked with the soil. They ate their food from earthenware bowls, inscribed their laws on clay tablets, dug their food from the soil and sheltered from the rain and wind in mud huts. These people were pagans who recognized their total dependence on the earth which they worshipped as a god or goddess. Nerthuis to the Teutons, En-lil among the Babylonians, Demeter for the Greeks and the Mexican Centeotl were all divinities of the earth. The Hindus gave thanks for the earth in their daily prayers: in the words of the *Atharva Veda*, 'O Earth, brown, black, red and multi-coloured, the firm Earth protected by Indra. On this earth may I stand unvanquished, unhurt, unstained.' In the Christian New Testament, rich use is made of homely farming analogies about planting and harvesting the land. This earthy approach was lost when Christianity came under the influence of Paul and the predominantly urban cultures of Rome and Greece. Nature was then relegated in importance and man took centre stage – a process which continues today.

During the nineteenth century there was a mass exodus from the country to the rapidly expanding industrial cities. In the process farm labourers boosted their earnings, but they lost not only the companionship which came from living in close rural communities but also their contact with the land. Some took refuge in drinking, hoping that alcohol would deaden their nostalgia, while others turned to crime. In an attempt to mitigate these social ills the British government passed the Allotment Act of 1908, which made it a duty for all local authorities to provide plots for the 'labouring poor'. Few councils responded to this decree until the First World War started, when the Board of Agriculture gained wide powers to requisition land. By 1917 over half a million plots had been created in parks, golf courses, tennis courts, abandoned gardens, rubbish tips and railway embankments. In some areas Sunday services were held on allotments so that gardeners could both work and worship. Allotments were again promoted during the Second World War, when the government launched a 'Dig for Victory' campaign. So successful was this initiative that private allotments generated 10 per cent of the nation's wartime food production. They enjoyed another surge of popularity in the 1960s, when thousands of families who were being rehoused in high-rise flats and felt the need for a patch of land which they could occupy and work. Now the emphasis has changed, and people are being urged to return to their allotment plots not to supplement the country's food supply but to improve the nation's health. A 1998 paper, 'The Future of Allotments', produced by a House of Commons select committee, calls upon government ministers to make these 'little lungs' part of their public health strategy because of their 'undisputed health benefits'.

Today in Britain there is a surfeit of reasonably priced food in the supermarkets, and yet there are still about 300,000 actively tended allotments, with an estimated 15,000 would-be gardeners waiting in line for a vacant lot. These patches of land are jealously guarded by their owners, to whom they represent not only freedom and exercise in the fresh air, but also the chance to return to a simpler way of life.

THE GAIA HYPOTHESIS

BIOLOGISTS BELIEVE THAT ABOUT 80 TO 90 PER CENT OF THE world's organisms are found in the soil, in a diverse mixture of bacteria, fungi, mites and nematodes. These subterranean creatures are essential for the continued existence of mankind and every other animal and plant. Earthworms, for instance, perform a vital service. Each one tunnels night and day, aerating the soil, breaking up and distributing masses of organic materials and drawing up 10 lb (4.5 kg) of worm-casts per year. No wonder they have been dubbed 'the Ploughs of God'! Since there are about 8 million earthworms in every acre of healthy soil, one can easily estimate the vast tonnage of earth they shift every day. Without these simple, sightless animals the soil would soon become compacted, sterile and airless and our planet would literally choke to death. 'It may be doubted whether there are any other animals which have played so important a part in the history of the world, as have these lowly organised creatures,' wrote Charles Darwin, who made a detailed study of their work.

The Soul Garden is tended by worms, and thousands of other unseen micro-organisms, rather than by human hands. Chemical fertilizers are not needed to feed the land and can even be positively harmful, for tests carried out by the US Department of Agriculture have shown that artificial nutrients such as ammonium sulphate damage the soil fungi and dramatically reduce the numbers of earthworms. If nourishment is required it can be provided by a surface layer of organic compost or manure, which produces an increase of about 13 per cent in the underlying worm population. A natural garden may need an initial dig to get rid of troublesome weeds, but after that it should not need digging or treatment with chemical nutrients and artificial pesticides. In its natural state the earth is stratified, rather like the human skin. On the outside it carries a layer of humus, which is a rich mixture of decaying vegetation and micro-organisms. This mantle serves a number of vital functions. It retains moisture, provides food for the earthworm population and encourages the growth of a wide range of essential bacteria and fungi. By binding the surface of the soil it reduces the risk of erosion, and by providing a loose blanket of insulation it helps to keep the soil warm in winter and cool in summer. No garden plot can be considered healthy if it is stripped of its humus covering, just as no human body can survive if too much of its skin coating is destroyed by burns. Every time we dig, hoe or rotavate we damage the earth by breaking up its outer layer of humus, and also run the risk of severing the more superficial rootlets of plants and shrubs.

There is no doubt in my mind of the superiority of the 'no-digging' method of gardening. This technique was championed by Dr Shelwell-Cooper, Director of the International Horticultural Bureau, who developed an experimental garden at Arkley Manor, Hertfordshire, where rose beds, vegetable gardens and flower borders remained consistently healthy and weed-free despite having been left untilled for years. Permanent crops should not be disturbed at all, according to Dr Shelwell-Cooper. All they need is hand weeding and yearly nourishment with a one-inch (2.5-cm) mulch of garden compost.

The Chinese are arguably the world's most successful farmers. They have been subjecting their soil to intensive cultivation for over four thousand years, and supporting more people per acre of land than any other nation. Yet their fields have not become infertile because they constantly feed them with a carefully composted mixture of vegetable refuse, animal dung and human excreta, using up every available scrap of organic waste.

Seeing how well the fertility of the land can be maintained without the help of the agrochemical industry, it is not difficult to accept the Gaia hypothesis. Named after Gaia, the Greek mother goddess of the earth, this theory holds that the earth is a complete and integrated organism, every part of which works in concert to sustain the health and harmony of the entire biosystem, just as the disparate cells and organs of an animal work together to ensure its survival. As a result of this integrated action planet earth maintains the optimum conditions for its survival, keeping a meticulous control of such things as the environmental temperature, the oxygen content of the air and the density of the ozone layer which protects us from excessive solar radiation.

A PLACE OF RENEWAL

SOMEWHERE WITHIN A SOUL GARDEN SPACE MUST BE FOUND FOR two or three compost heaps. These will serve two important functions. In the first place they will generate a constant supply of organic mulch to feed the land. Then, at a deeper, symbolic level they will provide a reminder of the endless cycle of birth, growth, decay, death and rebirth. The lifespan of individual organisms – whether buttercups, bees or human beings – may be exceedingly short, but life itself is eternal. So too are the raw materials of organic life. This is a lesson we learn every time we tend a compost heap, the very heat of which demonstrates that even in death there is vigorous life. Before our eyes, we witness the endless transformation of useless rubbish into vital nourishment.

In days gone by, dung heaps were far more prized than they are today. The people of ancient Jerusalem were prepared to travel to gardens which they built at some distance from their homes, in places like the Mount of Olives, because there was a law which forbade the use of manure on land which lay inside the walls of the Holy City. In the same way the Irish so treasured their stores of manure that they kept their dung heaps under constant surveillance, either right in front of their homes or even, occasionally, in one corner of their living rooms. Nowadays this respect is shown only by keen organic gardeners such as Prince Charles, who was amazed to find that his yew trees grew about a foot a year when he planted them in well-rotted manure. 'Witnessing the efficiency of muck was a very important lesson in my gardening education,' he writes, 'and I can safely say that whatever has been achieved at Highgrove has been done through well-rotted manure.'

The recipes for making compost are legion, but the basic principles are few. The process of organic decay needs warmth, oxygen, a modest degree of moisture and a mass of worms and bacteria. To provide the necessary organisms, the heap must be built on naked earth rather than on concrete slabs or wooden planks. And no chemicals, such as weedkillers, should be introduced into the pile which might harm their growth. The heap should be contained in a perforated frame, most commonly made from wooden slats, to allow the passage of air. For the same reason the stack should be made up of alternate layers of fine and coarse material – weeds interspersed with grass cuttings – so that air can permeate easily through the heap. If compacting occurs, a light forking can be used to aerate the congealed clods. Too much air, on the other hand, can slow down the process of decomposition, which makes it wise to trample down the heap from time to time. An old rug placed over the top of the pile can help to retain heat, and prevent excessive soaking from rain showers. Conversely, if the mound gets too dry, a light watering can help to keep it at an optimum moisture level. Temperatures of up to 49 degrees C (120 degrees F) may be generated within a compost heap, which speeds the process of decomposition and helps to kill weed seeds and destroy the organisms which give rise to plant disease. Nitrogenous accelerators, the simplest of which is urine, will increase the speed of bio-degeneration. Other alternatives are seaweed, poultry manure, horse dung and any of the proprietary compost accelerators. Even without these aids, the mere action of bacterial decomposition will increase the nitrogen content of the soil by up to 25 per cent. Within six to eighteen months the compost should be ready for spreading evenly over the garden, ideally so as to cover every patch of naked soil.

Only a true gardener knows the satisfaction which comes from creating a delicious mound of top-quality compost, which crumbles freely in the hand and looks like centuries-old peat, rich, dark, sweet-smelling, moist and friable. It's a primordial pleasure which rekindles awareness of our utter dependence on the natural cycle of regeneration and reuse. Every time we handle a lump of compost we are reminded that the earth is not dead, but pulsating with life.

When we live in towns we tend to equate earth with dirt and

grime, thinking of the dust we try to sweep from our streets, clean from our offices and banish from our homes. To a gardener, mud and muck are far more wholesome. It is the reflection of light through countless particles of dust which gives the sky its beautiful blue colour, and creates the glorious crimson sunsets. The gardener welcomes the feel of the earth and even loves its characteristic smell, especially when the parched soil receives a welcome shower of rain and exudes the scent of myriad traces of volatile oils. This perfume – known as petraclor – was recommended by Francis Bacon as a rejuvenant and a remedy for countless ills. He proposed it as a tonic for women, whom he urged to weed their gardens especially in the spring, when he claimed that the earth exuded its most energizing breath. Some people, and some animals, are more sensitive to this earthy smell than others. It is said that Sir Francis Drake could detect the presence of land by its smell long before it came into sight, and would set his course accordingly. Other skippers had less sensitive noses and so followed the ancient practice of the Polynesian islanders, who took pigs with them on their long sea voyages in the sure knowledge that after weeks at sea the creatures would become excited when they caught their first whiff of terra firma, even if the land was well beyond the immediate horizon.

THE CYCLE OF LIFE

LIVING CLOSE TO THE EARTH MAKES US MORE AWARE OF THE endless cycle of life, death, decay and rebirth. We see leaf buds forming at the end of winter. We watch the foliage unfurl in the spring and then turn colour and fall in the autumn. But when does the life of a leaf come to an end? Is it the moment when it falls from the tree, when it is turned into humus in the soil, or when its raw materials are absorbed and used to nourish a growing tree? In a garden we learn that life does not start and stop, it is a continuing process. Nowadays we talk of 'the creation' as the instant when life began, but it was a basic tenet of early Christian theology that creation was not a once-and-for-all event but a continuing cycle, an endless process known as the *creatio continua*. Scientists know that matter cannot be created or destroyed, it can only be transmuted into a different form. Some kind of reincarnation takes place when organisms die, whether it is the rebirth of souls or merely the molecular re-cycling of cellular material.

When we wish to remember the dead we create memorial gardens, which serve to remind us that when we commit our loved ones to their earthly graves we are in the presence not only of death but also of life. Today death has become a taboo subject. The Victorians talked about death all the time but never mentioned sex. We talk constantly about sex, but rarely mention death. Death has become a medical procedure rather than a family rite of passage. We don't lay out the dead as our grand-parents did, we hand the responsibility to an undertaker. But I believe that gardeners, possibly through their close relationship with the earth, find it easier to come to terms with matters of life and death. When I die I want some of my ashes to be sprinkled on my latest compost heap to reaffirm the principle of biological reincarnation and to demonstrate that whatever lived once can be recycled and live again. Where people die, poppies grow. That is the lesson of the compost heap.

Some people decry the amount of urban land devoted to cemeteries, saying that they would rather see the space used for housing. 'Land for the Living' is their battle cry. But cemeteries have proved among the finest spots for preserving the flora and fauna of cities and villages. Half of London's contemporary gardens and parks were built on land that was once burial grounds and plague pits, and in rural areas the churchyards which have been untouched by plough and pesticides for centuries now provide some of the best natural habitats for endangered meadow plants. Many communities are currently engaging bands of volunteers to develop churchyards as wildlife havens. If you're short of garden space, why not approach the vicar with an offer to turn the local graveyard into an attractive garden of remembrance?

The soil contains nutrients and micro-organisms which are essential for the perpetuation of the food chain on which our lives depend. Animals cannot live without plants, and plants cannot survive without nitrogen-fixing bacteria, and the host of other organisms which oxidize the inorganic chemicals in the soil and make them available for absorption and plant growth. Yet we constantly spray the earth with poisons which impair its health. Our avowed aim is to kill selectively those plants and organisms which we, in our infinite wisdom, deem to be unwanted. But in the process we destroy everything within our line of fire. Too often we give way to the urge to control, and demonstrate our power not through our capacity to nurture but through our ability to destroy.

In 1972 a statement was issued called *A Blueprint for Survival*, which had the signed support of thirty-seven of the world's leading scientists. It said: 'There are half a million man-made chemicals in use today, yet we cannot predict the behaviour or properties of the greater part of them (either singly or in combination) once they are released into the environment. We know, however, that the combined effects of pollution and habitat destruction menace the survival of no less than 280 mammal, 350 bird and 200,000 plant species.' When we spray our gardens with herbicides, pesticides and fungicides, intending to clear dandelions from our lawns, aphids from our fruit trees and stinging nettles from our shrub borders, we naively believe that we are improving things. We forget that in killing aphids, nettles and dandelions we are destroying part of the ecological nexus on which our lives depend. When we destroy aphids, we also exterminate the ladybirds which are their natural predators. When we eliminate stinging nettles, we destroy the breeding ground of butterflies, which we need to encourage within a Soul Garden. Without a generous supply of bugs and insects how can we expect birds to nest and feed their young? We should be as careful with the poisons we put on our gardens as we are with those we put in our mouths, for they are all part of the same food chain. There is no place for pesticides in a Soul Garden, which is a sanctuary where all organisms can and should work together in a state of happy symbiosis.

THE ANCIENT ART OF GEOTHERAPY

IN A GARDEN WE LEARN TO APPRECIATE OUR TOTAL DEPENDENCE ON micro-organisms, rather than to fear them simply because one or two rogue bacteria can give rise to human sickness. At one time it was a traditional country remedy to apply an earth poultice to heal an infected wound or graze. Danish peasants believed that a whitlow could be healed by thrusting the finger into the ground, and family doctors urged youngsters to use clay packs as a cure for acne. These may be valid practices, for mud and soil are now known to have antibiotic properties. Professor Selman A. Walksman discovered streptomycin in 1946 after analysing thousands of separate soil samples, and another research team, led by Dr Benjamin Duggar, studied some thirty thousand samples before finding the precursors of aureomycin in earth taken from a site adjoining a cemetery.

Our resistance to disease may be enhanced by regular association with the soil. Such contact with the countless bacteria in the earth is prophylactic, because it triggers a defensive immune reaction which helps to raise our resistance to infection and reduce our liability to allergies and auto-immune disease. This was the theory of Sir Almoth Wright, who argued that it was better to stimulate the body's own phagocytes than to rely on artificial antiseptics and bactericidal agents. He was a close friend of George Bernard Shaw, who caricatured his belief in *The Doctor's Dilemma* (1911), where people are constantly being urged to 'Stimulate the phagocytes!' to improve their health and enhance their resistance to disease. The immune system doesn't develop adequately if children are brought up on super-sterilized food and dosed with antibiotics whenever they suffer a minor infection.

Gardeners quickly come to accept that a peck of dirt hurts nobody. Now it seems that dirt may even be therapeutic. This theory was advanced recently by two immunologists from University College, London who published a medical paper, 'Give us this day, our daily germs', which followed the theme of Almoth

Wright and argued that bacterial conditions today can be too sterile for our own good, which might help to explain why eczema, asthma and hay fever have doubled in the last twenty-five years. These are now considered to be 'diseases of the advantaged' because they are more prevalent among children born in affluent surroundings than among those who grow up in shanty towns and slums. Most of the mycobacteria in the soil are not only harmless but positively beneficial. Every time we come into contact with them we strengthen our immune systems. In an experiment researchers succeeded in curing mice of an allergy to egg-white by making them inhale the mycobacteria obtained from soil samples. This success has led to attempts to develop a human anti-allergy vaccine made from the distilled extracts of soil.

A well-nourished soil also contains a varied supply of minerals – iron, magnesium, copper, zinc, manganese and selenium. These micro-nutrients are taken up by the plants we grow and become an important ingredient of the food we eat. People living on iodine-deficient soils are prone to develop myxoedema, because iodine is essential for the formation of thyroxine, the hormone manufactured by the thyroid gland. To this extent 'we are what we eat'. To compensate for these deficiencies some people have adopted the custom of eating mineral-rich earth and clay, a widespread practice known as geophagy. In Africa, alluvial mud is eaten mainly by anaemic children and pregnant women. However, the clay eating stops the moment blood levels of iron are raised by the administration of iron-containing pills. This custom is not limited to the people of the Third World; early in the twentieth century there was a vogue in Europe for eating Vitae Ore, a mud which contained a high percentage of ferric salts. This panacea was said to turn tired and jaded patients into people with 'vigour to spare, men with breezy personalities and women whose warm blood and feminine grace captures all hearts'. Before the advent of Vitae Ore it was thought that people who ate mud were mad – afterwards they were reclassified as health enthusiasts, which some consider another form of insanity! But it is not necessary to eat dirt, or wallow in mud, to enjoy the psychological benefits of geotherapy. Merely working the land is enough to foster an increase in physical well-being.

HOME GROUND

IN OUR HEADLONG DASH AROUND THE GLOBAL VILLAGE, WE sometimes require the bedrock security of having our feet planted on terra firma. We still feel the need for a patch of earth we can call our own, where we can establish a true pied-à-terre. Our tenure of this patch gives us a sense of pride and, indeed, land ownership has always conferred power. For centuries there were only two social classes, the gentry which owned the land and the peasantry which worked it. The first had power – to vote, to levy manorial taxes and to administer justice – while the second was socially impotent. Legislation has gradually blurred this distinction and brought about a more equitable distribution of land, but we still experience a feeling of satisfaction when we survey our personal fiefdom, even if it is simply a modest allotment or small town garden. Whatever its size, it is *our* land, and part of *our* native country.

Charles A. Reich, in his bestselling book *The Greening of America*, spoke of the revolution in consciousness which was sweeping through the United States at the start of the 1970s. This change in outlook, he said, promised 'a new and enduring wholeness and beauty – a renewed relationship of man to himself, to other men, to society, to nature and to the land'. That revolution failed to develop to the extent that Reich had hoped, because everyone looked to someone else to bring about the change. If we want to preserve the environment, we must put it into private hands. It may be a sad reflection on modern society, but it is nevertheless true to say that 'Everybody's property is nobody's property'. Our greatest hope of achieving the greening of the industrialized world is to give everyone the responsibility of enhancing the beauty of their own gardens. To motivate this revolutionary change we should regard ourselves, not as the outright owners of our garden plots, but merely as their custodians. The Native Americans found it amazing that immigrant settlers thought they could *buy* huge tracts of countryside. To them the land was not a commodity which could be bought or sold, any more than one could purchase the air or the sun's rays. This belief was beautifully expressed in a letter Chief Seathl wrote to the President of the United States in 1885: 'Every part of this earth is sacred to my people. Every shining pine needle, every sandy shore, every mist in the dark woods, every clearing and humming insect is holy in the memory and experience of my people.' Some doubt has been cast on the authenticity of this letter, but it well expresses the beliefs of most pastoral people. We don't inherit land from our ancestors, we hold it in trust for future generations.

Even the simplest organisms appear to feel happier, and more secure, when they are within the bounds of their own territory. Planarium worms take twice as long to settle down and begin eating in unfamiliar surroundings as they do when they are on their native feeding grounds. In the same way, just as sports teams are more successful when playing at home, so wild animals win far more battles when they are fighting on their native terrain. We too are territorial animals. In fact it has been argued that men have a stronger bond with the land on which they walk than with the women with whom they sleep, for while millions have died in defence of their native lands, very few have died to protect their wives and lovers.

Nowadays this bond with the land is weakening because we lead such nomadic lives. One in five Americans now moves home every year and this rapid rate of relocation means it is difficult to develop a sense of 'home'. People may travel for pleasure and to overcome boredom, but the freedom to move is no substitute for the comfort and security which comes from settled ownership of a plot of land. Even those individuals who are forced by their jobs to lead the lives of corporate gypsies invariably have a yen to establish a more permanent base.

People in the past had an awareness of place, both socially and geographically. Many were buried in the same village as their parents and grandparents, amid the community in which they were born and bred and spent their entire working lives. Houses and cottages were handed down from father to son for generations. Some people, of course, were driven from these settled communities because they held non-conformist political or religious beliefs, and when such disruption occurred the emigrants generally lost no time in staking a private claim to territory overseas. When the Pilgrim Fathers and their families landed in Massachusetts Bay, they immediately built a protective stockade around their homes and provided each house with its own garden plot. In this way they clearly defined the heartland of the new community and also the boundaries of the private territory of each individual family.

This desire to establish one's home ground is almost certainly an atavistic drive. Dogs mark their territory by leaving urine traces around its perimeter, birds sing on prominent branches around its boundaries and grizzly bears make warning scratches on conspicuous trees at its borders. We are motivated by the same instinct, and delineate our home territory with fences, walls and hedges. If we are to feel totally comfortable and secure within a Soul Garden it needs to be surrounded by a reasonably clear boundary.

Studies of human spatial behaviour show that we recognize certain fairly consistent boundary limits. For instance, we feel uneasy if people come within eighteen inches of us, unless it is an intimate encounter with someone we love. Most other personal encounters take place within a range of eighteen inches to four feet, a distance which varies from culture to culture. Psychologists also recognize more distant boundaries, which they place in three categories: public territory (beaches, parks, trains and restaurants), secondary territory (social clubs and other spaces reserved for the use of members) and primary territory (a home and garden). We defend our rights to all these domains, but none so jealously as our right to exclusive possession of our house and garden. Any unauthorized encroachment on that space is often taken as a serious personal affront.

We are led to believe that the new communication technology will create a global village which will break down these traditional boundaries. This is a rash prediction, for it totally ignores the strength of our territorial instinct. A far more likely scenario is that the global village will become so vast and impersonal that we will hanker even more for our own private space. Two other factors will augment this trend. Travel in the future will almost certainly become increasingly congested and troublesome, placing an added premium on entertainment in and around the home. In addition, the development of electronic communications will make it easier for people to live and work at home, a privilege once reserved for writers, artists and craftsmen. George Bernard Shaw did most of his writing in the garden of his home in Ayot St Lawrence, where he built a writing hut shielded from the main house by a screen of trees, and mounted on wheels so that it could be turned to face the sun throughout the day. Claude Monet also found he could work better in a rural environment, so in 1890 he left Paris and bought a plot of land in the village of Giverny. Here he created a Japanese water garden, complete with lily pond, oriental bridge, bamboos and overhanging willow trees, which is now open to the public. His new private territory served as his workplace for the remainder of his life, and provided the subject matter of some of his most famous paintings.

NO PLACE LIKE HOME

THE MORE TRANSIENT AND STRESSFUL OUR LIVES, THE MORE WE need to foster our roots in the earth. Our home ground gives us a feeling of security, and strangely it also contributes to our sense of personal identity. This garden is *mine* but, in a variety of subtle ways, this garden is also *me*. We often speak of the garden as an extension of the house; more than that, it is an extension of our individual personalities. We express ourselves in the way we design, plant, tend and use our gardens. In *Why We Garden: Cultivating a sense of place*, J. Nollman argued that when we create a garden we develop a nurturing partnership with nature, which generates an intimate bond with one particular patch of land. It is that sense of place, he said, which introduces the spiritual dimension into gardening.

This is also the essence of the Chinese art of *feng shui*, which has been defined as 'the art of finding one's place'. This ancient practice, dating back over seven thousand years, regards mankind as the essential link between heaven and earth. According to *feng shui* experts, human beings are happier, healthier and more successful when they give proper thought to the spatial alignment of their homes and gardens. They recommend, for one thing, that gardens should be enclosed by a fence in order to provide protection for the house. This rule was carefully followed in the siting of the Forbidden City, the seat of the Chinese emperors in Beijing, which is surrounded by an undulating river and set just inside the city's outermost walls.

Many animals show a well-developed homing instinct. Green turtles make a hazardous 1,400-mile journey across the Atlantic Ocean in order to return to their breeding grounds in the Ascension Islands. The elvers which can be caught at the bottom of my garden have made the great trek from the Sargasso Sea to reach their home in the headwaters of the river Severn, where they will mature for a few years before returning to the Gulf of Mexico. This homing instinct is an integral part of the territorial drive. Like elastic, its pull is exerted only when its points of attachment are stretched. We may not experience this calling when we are home with our kith and kin, but its force is expressed – as homesickness, nostalgia or exaggerated patriotism – the moment we are exiled. That feeling, known to the Welsh as *herith*, is particularly strong when we throw down roots, establish a home and nurture a personal garden plot.

The English writer Hugh Massingham made this discovery relatively late in life. In his early years he had always lived in rented homes and had therefore had little chance to develop a 'sense of place'. Then he became the owner of some land in Horton-cum-Studley, a village in the Cotswolds. In *This Plot of Earth*, he related how he slowly and determinedly transformed his small patch of British soil into a delightful self-sufficiency garden. 'I know that the act of becoming an owner-occupier of a piece of English land proved an educative force in responsibility and obligation which was one of the greatest "point-events" of my whole life,' he wrote. 'As a result of land belonging to me I found that I belonged to the land.' This yearning to colonize a minute portion of planet earth has grown stronger in society as a whole in recent years, perhaps as a reaction to a growing loss of privacy.

THE HUMAN ZOO

WE CANNOT FUNCTION PROPERLY WITHOUT THE COMPANY AND support of other sentient beings, and yet to remain healthy we also need a regular supply of solitude and seclusion. When animals are herded together in cages they suffer symptoms of mental distress which they never experience in the wild. Autopsy studies carried out at the Philadelphia Zoo Gardens revealed a ten- to twenty-fold increase in arteriosclerosis in mammals and birds over a forty-year period. This was attributed in large measure to 'social pressures' resulting from an increase in the density of the animal populations in the zoo. In their natural state, animals inhabit a personal territory where they are free from all forms of social interference. When they are in close confinement in a zoo they lose the protection of this comforting buffer zone. They cannot escape from rivals, keep irritating cohorts at bay or take an occasional breather from the endless erotic arousal of male and female encounters. This abnormal social crowding leads to increased friction, fighting and hyper-sexuality. Similar changes are seen in humans when they are closely confined. Sailors imprisoned for months in nuclear submarines are subject to moodiness, depression and hyper-irritability. The same symptoms arose in polar explorers when they were forced to live in close proximity during the long Arctic winters; the syndrome was often referred to as 'expedition choler'.

This introduces one of the great dilemmas of Soul Garden design, a subject which is fully resolved only in the final chapter of this book. Gardens are ideal places for people to meet and share food and drink or play games. In cities, by tradition, the main discourse between neighbours took place over the garden wall. Those social needs must still be met, and yet at the same time we must aim whenever possible to create gardens which also provide a degree of privacy. This can sometimes be done, in even the smallest urban garden, by constructing secluded arbours, where we can quietly retire to meditate without risk of being overlooked.

Freedom is rightly prized as one of the inalienable rights of people living in liberal democracies. Despite the growth of planning rules and regulations, our homes are still our private territory. Here we can live with a great degree of independence, shaping our own environment, growing our own food and creating our own pastimes. When we do this we realize how little we need to satisfy our basic requirements. The inexorable expansion of trade today depends on creating artificial needs, but you can't sell anything to a contented man or woman. If you're happy in your garden, what need do you have for external luxuries? If you're satisfied with a simple picnic on the lawn, why should you patronize fashionable restaurants? If you can get your fun nurturing a row of broad beans, why should you crave the ersatz entertainment of cinemas and night clubs?

You cannot dominate independent, self-sufficient people. This was proved during the French Revolution, when the Basque peasants were urged to join the rebels against the landowning aristocracy. They showed no inclination to join the insurrection because they were already free and perfectly content with their lot. They were not serfs, for they each owned a small patch of land. '*Ici, tous les gens sont propriétaires*' was their famous response. 'Here, we are all landowners.'

Even a small town garden can be enough to create the necessary feeling of land ownership and personal freedom. Town planners may think it impracticable to offer everyone a private plot within an overcrowded modern city, but the truth is that terraced houses with modest-sized gardens can be built to the same high densities as tower blocks. According to one calculation, every adult in Britain could occupy a house and small garden, with all these homes contained within a radius of thirty-five miles of the centre of London. Unfortunately, modern towns are designed not to meet the needs of people but to satisfy the growing demands of cars. In Georgian times the houses of London were built around spacious, cobbled squares which were wide enough to allow the turning and parking of horse-drawn carriages. As the city grew, the gardens of these grand houses were turned into building plots. To compensate for the loss of trees and shrubs, the local residents got together to dig up the squares and turn them into communal gardens. But while these squares are delightful amenities, they are no substitute for the security of a truly private garden.

Utopia is not a state of mind or a way of life, it is quint-essentially a place. (The term was coined by Thomas More from the Greek words *eu topos*, meaning 'the good place'.) When the Persians built their early town gardens they aimed to create mini-utopias enclosed within high walls, providing cool and leafy oases in a dry, barren land. Many Christians shared a similar ambition and treasured icons of the Virgin Mary sitting in a garden, surrounded by songbirds and roses, with a fountain or well to represent the Spring of Life. Once again the emphasis was on the enclosure of the garden space and in fact one of the many names for the Virgin Mary is *hortus conclusus*, 'the enclosed garden'. The pagan religions had a similar concept. The Romans worshipped a god of enclosures, and believed that structures were sacred if they served the function of marking divisions. This was especially true of the walls, fences and hedges which divided the land of neighbours. Boundaries were clearly delineated by marker stones which it was sacrilege to move. As Plato put it: 'Our first law should be this: Let no person touch the bounds that separate his field from that of his neighbour.' The same point was made by James Madison, an early US president who played a major part in drawing up the American Constitution and Bill of Rights. He claimed that the protection of property rights was 'the first object of government'.

A PRIVATE VIEW

PLANTSMEN AND HORTICULTURISTS ARE SOMETIMES SO CLOSE TO their subject that they fail to recognize the psychological importance of gardening. This significance was not lost on some of the great architects of the past, such as Paxton, Vanbrugh, Kent and Chambers, who were among the most influential landscape gardeners of the eighteenth century. The same is true of many outstanding architects of recent times, such as Frank Lloyd Wright and Le Corbusier, who took an essentially ecological approach to house design. Frank Lloyd Wright realized that domestic buildings met the need for emotional security and refuge, and so constructed 'prairie houses' in which his clients were encouraged to retreat from the elements 'as into a cave'. In many of these buildings he incorporated trees and plants, so that their occupants could enter their sanctuaries and not be divorced from nature. Le Corbusier took this a stage further, constructing houses which permitted a direct sensory experience of the elements. He loved the great outdoors, in particular the spacious vistas he saw when he trekked through the Jura, and tried to incorporate the elements of sunlight, clouds, wind and stars into his house designs.

This draws attention to another core dilemma of garden design. To satisfy our need for seclusion and safety we may feel the need to enclose our gardens with high walls, hedges and fences, but at the same time we want to enjoy panoramic views. We would like to see, but not be seen. These twin needs can be met by building our homes on hills and mountain tops, which were the chosen sites for many of the early temples, palaces and castles. Few people today can hope to occupy these lofty heights, and so they have to create their own views, which at the same time do not compromise their equal need for security and seclusion.

When fashion designer Oscar de la Renta wanted to create a traditional English garden at his Connecticut home, he was warned by his garden designer Russell Page: 'A garden has to have walls and to build walls would be to obstruct the view.' Being a determined character, the designer went ahead with his plans. With Page's help, he built a glorious garden with enclosed 'rooms' which nevertheless enjoyed extensive views over the neighbouring Litchfield Hills. In the eighteenth century a number of tricks were used to provide panoramic views without compromising the security of a garden plot. Artificial hillocks and mounds were constructed to give views above perimeter fences. *Clairs-voyées* (openings often filled with ornamental grilles) were inset into walls to provide restricted glimpses of the surrounding countryside, and ha-has or boundary ditches were built so that cattle and people could be barred from the private space of a garden without obstructing the view of the surrounding scenery. William Beckford, the eccentric English collector, found another way of satisfying his need for total seclusion combined with unobstructed views. He inherited five hundred acres of land on which he set out to create a fantastic building – Fonthill Abbey, one of the first and grandest examples of Gothic Revival architecture. But he desperately needed privacy, to escape the endless gossip and censure which his private life evoked, so he surrounded the estate with a high, fortified wall. Since the enclosure obstructed his view, he then built a 276-foot tower, from which he could view the surrounding countryside.

Privacy of this order is particularly important for people in the public eye. When Prince Charles bought Highgrove House its gardens were surrounded by a stone wall of little more than shoulder height. To provide a better defence against prying eyes and telephoto lenses, he immediately set about raising the height of the wall, behind which he planted a tall yew hedge. Only when this perimeter fence was in place did he start the creation of his private garden, into which he has sunk his heart and soul. The same need for privacy motivated Queen Elizabeth when she bought a home in Surrey for the Duchess of York. The house had a well-established five-acre garden surrounded by a thirty-foot brick wall.

While we will almost certainly have no place for such a massive structure, we would still do well to plan our gardens so that they are secluded and secure. At the same time we need to preserve pleasing views. The art is to use trees and shrubs to obscure unsightly objects in the immediate vicinity, and open up selective gaps so that we can enjoy the surrounding scenery.

THE INNER PILGRIMAGE

IT IS NEVER TOO EARLY, NOR TOO LATE, TO NURTURE A SENSE OF place. If children are to develop a love of gardening they should be given their own patch of land at the earliest possible moment.

Even toddlers need their personal space. 'A lucky child will be allowed, as I was, to take over a patch of the family garden,' writes Elspeth Thompson of the *Sunday Telegraph*. 'Clear boundaries are a must: if a low tub, or small, self-contained bed is not an option, make a low wall or edge the borders with shells or pebbles.' Old stagers, too, need contact with the earth. History is full of examples of eminent people – soldiers, industrialists and statesmen – who have retired from the turmoil of public life to enjoy the quiet seclusion of a private garden. A typical example is Montgomery Cowley, a distinguished soldier who fought for King Charles at the Battle of Marston Moor and later became a successful merchant. Eventually he decided to retire from what he called 'the tumult and business of the world', to devote himself to the twin solaces of creating a garden and writing poetry. These proved the all-absorbing focus of his twilight years. God gave man a garden even before he gave him a wife, he argued in his poem 'The Garden': 'God the first Garden made, and the first city, Cain.'

We feel more secure when we rediscover our grass roots and recognize our total dependence on nature. This journey of self-discovery starts, not with a pilgrimage to the Holy Land or a trek to a monastery in Tibet, but when we obtain and start to cultivate a private patch of land. Here, on a modest allotment or in a tiny town garden, we can find happiness and peace through enjoying what Browning described as the 'good gigantic smile o' the brown old earth'.

People are rarely happier than when they are
cultivating their own plot of land. This gives us a
sense of belonging, of being in control and of personal
responsibility. Most primitive cultures observed myths
which honoured the earth as the primordial mother of
the human race, and gardening is a powerful continuation
of this ancient tradition. When we cultivate the soil we
pay tribute to Ceres, the Roman goddess of growing
vegetation also known as the alma mater or 'nourishing
mother'. By performing the simple, atavistic rites of a
gardener we re-establish our grass roots, come down to
earth and draw strength from having our feet firmly
planted on terra firma.

    We are essentially territorial animals, and just as
sports teams have a far greater chance of
success when playing at home, so we feel
happier and more secure when we are
standing on our own plot of land. This is
especially true when the land is surrounded by
a protective hedge or fence. A Soul Garden is designed to
meet fundamental human needs by providing a secure,
enclosed personal space where individuals can re-establish
their primeval connections with Mother Earth.

CHAPTER THREE

A Pagan Paradise

'He who knows what sweets and virtues are in the ground, the plants, the waters, the heavens, and how to come at these enchantments – is the rich and royal man.'

RALPH WALDO EMERSON

*G*ARDENERS ARE LIKE LANDSCAPE PAINTERS. THEIR canvas is the soil, their paints the vast array of living flowers, trees and shrubs. They get their inspiration by studying nature. Russell Page, one of the most prolific and successful garden designers of the twentieth century, trained to be an artist but quickly turned his attention to creating horticultural masterpieces. His inspiration came from his contact with nature. As a boy raised in the English countryside, he spent most of his time wandering through woods and fields, beside streams and along meandering country paths. 'I knew every hedgerow in detail,' he recalled, 'the texture of the leaves and twigs, the visual effects of changing skies, the varying scents of leaf and flower, the nature of the soils and the stones, to the point that all were part of me and I of them.' This has been the education of all the great landscape gardeners. They have created gardens which have been wild, varied, irregular, random, luxuriant and mystical, because this is the sum and substance of the natural landscape they have observed and sought to replicate in miniature within a horticultural framework.

When people create gardens they give expression to their personalities. Some favour formality and symmetry because they feel more comfortable when they are imposing order upon their immediate environment. Others are happier in chaotic surroundings. The Soul Garden lies somewhere between these two extremes. It is contrived, but at the same time informal and irregular rather than strictly disciplined. Straight lines, wherever they occur, are signs of authority and regimentation. Animal tracks are never straight, nor are country lanes. When the

Romans invaded Britain they replaced the ancient, meandering tracks of the Celts and Anglo-Saxons with straight highways. Although these were appropriate for an invading military power, their remnants today seem artificial and incongruous since they follow a ruler-straight course across a rural landscape where everything else is irregular and curved. European cities developed wide straight streets, known in the fifteenth century as *viae militares*, to aid the flow of troops and to provide for military displays. The same plumb-straight malls appeared in public parks, to provide places for people to promenade and display their fashionable clothes, but they left no nooks and alleys for romance and intrigue. Many modern cities are built on strict grid or radial plans, for ease of management and control, but to most eyes they lack the beauty, romance and charm of the old cities criss-crossed by crooked alleys and winding lanes.

If a garden is to mirror nature it must be varied, irregular, random and wild. Such an effect can be created in a window box as well as in the rolling acres of a country estate, simply by employing strands of ivy and trailing plants to break the rigid, rectangular outline of the container. Cities and houses may incorporate straight lines, but never gardens. This accords with the teaching of the Chinese *feng shui* masters who claimed that straight lines should be avoided in a garden because they interrupt the flow of the life force or *chi*.

Following the oriental example, the British tried to make their gardens natural and wild. The overriding aim was to make them *sharadwadgi*, a term derived in the seventeenth century from the Japanese horticultural expression *soro-wa-ji*, meaning 'not being symmetrical'. This preference for gentle, undulating curves rather than sharp angles can also be explained in terms of aesthetic appreciation, for tests have revealed that viewing angles and curves provokes a totally different emotional response. Psychologists showed a representative group of five hundred people a variety of lines, arranged either as wave forms or as sharp zigzags, and asked them to describe the moods the various lines induced. The responses showed a remarkable consistency: the soft waves were described as 'quiet', 'playful', 'merry', 'serene' and 'gentle', and the sharp angles as 'harsh', 'furious', 'agitating' and 'powerful'. If we want our gardens to create a mood of gentle serenity we must ensure that they are filled with smooth curves rather than harsh angles. It was, of course, these principles which inspired the Romantic movement of the eighteenth century, when wealthy British landowners set out to create gardens which mimicked the landscapes depicted by the French painters Claude Lorraine and Nicolas Poussin – gardens steeped in romance, complete with follies, grottoes, Roman temples and mock-medieval ruins.

THE GRAND TOUR

ARISTOCRATIC YOUNG MEN OF THE SEVENTEENTH AND EIGHTEENTH centuries completed their education by making a grand tour of Europe. Here they admired the wild, dramatic scenery but often heaped scorn on what they regarded as the outdated formality of the Franco-Italian gardens with their neat parterres, regular knot gardens and close-clipped topiary hedges. Joseph Addison, the English poet and essayist, was typical of his generation. As a young man he undertook a two-year tour of Europe and was thrilled by the beauty of the rocky valley of the river Tiber and the majestic views of Mount Vesuvius. These stimulated his aesthetic sense far more than the artificial grounds of the grand chateaux and villas. Alexander Pope, a fellow poet, was of the same opinion. The delightful garden he created in Twickenham, on the outskirts of London, was one of the very first to be designed in the new, natural style. In his 'Epistle to Lord Burlington' he gives clear directions for creating a romantic garden, the key instruction being 'In all let Nature never be forgot.' Apart from the wood and stone structure of patios, archways, terraces, fountains, seats and statues, Pope wrote, the natural garden should appear to have arisen of its own accord, neither conceived by human mind nor touched by human hand, 'discover'd, not devis'd'.

It has often been said that Britain's greatest contribution to culture has been the invention of the landscape garden, exemplified by such horticultural wonderlands as Glendurgan in Cornwall, Montacute in Somerset, Stourhead in Wiltshire, Hidcote in the Cotswolds and Winkworth in Surrey. This is rightly a cause for national pride; on the other hand, Britain also played a major part in destroying the whole concept of landscape gardening through a nineteenth-century obsession with plant collecting. During the buccaneering days of colonial expansion, British adventurers travelled the world to plant the Union Jack on foreign shores and to bring back a booty of exotic flowers and shrubs. These new species were proudly displayed like museum exhibits in royal parks and botanical gardens. The wealthy collected rare plants as avidly as they amassed expensive objets d'art and their gardens became exhibition halls rather than natural beauty spots. A snobbery developed during Victorian times when the flowers which were popular with labourers and factory workers, such as auriculas, pinks and pansies, became decried as 'mechanic's flowers'. No refined household would find space for such hackneyed specimens. They preferred less commonplace plants, like blue roses, miniature daffodils and double philadelphus, and whenever possible opted for novelty varieties that were *variegatus*, *pendens* or *tortuosa*.

While this urge to collect, assemble and classify plants may be an enjoyable pastime – every bit as satisfying as collecting stamps or matchbox labels – it is not a necessary part of Soul Gardening. Beauty can be found as readily in a simple pansy as in a rare orchid. If anyone new to landscape gardening should want a simple maxim to govern their work, they would be well advised to adopt the aphorism of Thoreau: 'True art is our expression of our love for nature.'

THE WATERS OF LIFE

THE ANCIENT GREEKS BELIEVED THAT THE COSMOS CONSISTED OF four basic elements – earth, air, fire and water. Each of these fundamental ingredients was worshipped in pagan rites and celebrations, and deserves to receive some form of homage in a Soul Garden. From a gardener's point of view the most important of these elements is probably earth, which we have already considered in the previous chapter. Plants cannot grow without soil, but equally they cannot flourish without water, an element which always featured prominently in the pagan gardens of Greece and Rome.

When the Romans established themselves in Britain in the early centuries of the first millennium, they built a number of palatial villas, surrounded by gardens filled with formal pools, cascading streams, irrigated terraces and carefully constructed spring-heads which served as shrines to their pagan gods.

Water features were equally prominent in the 'paradise' gardens of the Arabs and Persians, so much so that it is impossible to think of the magnificent Alhambra Palace in Granada without its profusion of fountains and ponds. Every one of its walled patios and courtyards is adorned with water features, fed by a constant stream flowing along the man-made *acequia* or Grand Canal which links the Alhambra Palace to the neighbouring hills. Even in the height of summer the gardens are cool and green, and filled with the refreshing sound of trickling water. 'Water', an Arab poet wrote, 'is the music of the Alhambra.'

The sound of running water is soothing to the ear, providing the 'white noise' which helps to block out the cacophony of urban traffic. Some of our happiest moments are spent beside water, splashing in the bath as babies, fishing for tiddlers as children, swimming in the sea as adults. Countless religious ceremonies, ranging from pagan rain dances to the Hindu custom of bathing in the sacred river Ganges and the Christian rite of baptism, acknowledge the mystical significance of water. Indeed, water is the very stuff of life, a fact recognized by the Japanese who, in their written texts, employ a symbol for 'water' which is almost indistinguishable from their ideogram for 'eternity'.

We are at home with water. Our own bodies are 75 per cent water. Before we were born the watery cavern of our mother's womb was our home and the soothing lapping of the amniotic fluid was the first sound we heard. Our ancestors were aquatic creatures, and even today the human foetus passes through a developmental stage when it shows clear evidence of fish-like gills. This aquatic heritage is deeply embedded in our psyche and appears in many global myths and rituals. Water has long been associated with fertility. Wells are female symbols, holes sunk into the body of Mother Earth, rich sources of life and nourishment. The Roman armies built wells wherever they travelled in Europe, not only to ensure a safe source of drinking water, but also to provide shrines for the worship of the water goddess. Throughout Britain the remains have been found of many of these holy wells, especially in the Celtic lands of Ireland and Wales, where over four thousand have been identified. One common country custom was for women to dance round these wells, with skirts raised, to increase their fertility. The popularity of symbolic wells in modern suburban gardens may be attributed to these primordial water rites.

Water in a garden is never static. One day it may take the form of a heavy downpour of rain, while the next it bathes everything in a gentle, early morning mist. In the summer it reveals itself as a heat haze, in the winter as hail, sleet or snow. A garden which incorporates a water feature is never dull. Water represents boundless energy, which we observe in the massive, chaotic force of tidal waves and in the harnessed power of water mills and hydraulic power plants. Water is the well-spring of life. The water falling from a fountain is always the same, yet always in motion. This was the discovery of Heraclitus, the Greek philosopher, who lived throughout his life by a sinuous, ever-changing river called the Meander. This was the inspiration for one of his most famous aphorisms: 'No man can step into the same river twice.' In an elemental garden we are reminded that everything in nature is in a state of flux and yet also possesses an inherent solidity and permanence.

UPON THIS ROCK

IN THE SECOND PHASE OF HIS LIFE THE PSYCHIATRIST CARL JUNG became fascinated by the universality of legends and myths. He studied the folklore of East and West and found that certain archetypal symbols – water, fire, standing stones, caves and dragons – were so universal that they could not have been spread simply by word of mouth. Instead he concluded that they must represent primordial memories deeply embedded in the consciousness of the human race. They were evidence of the collective unconscious, a timeless psychic continuum which he conceptualized as connecting all sentient beings at a level below that of the conscious thought processes of the individual man or woman. When we are aware of these symbols we at once become part of something which is greater and older than our tiny, temporal selves. Gardening connects us with this archetypal world, for it brings us into intimate contact with some of the most powerful and evocative prehistoric memories involving water, earth and stone.

Gardens need to feature far more than flowers and shrubs if they are to help us maintain our connection with this rich common heritage. Intuitively we feel the need for structures which provide a sense of solidity, strength and permanence. All the great gardens of the world contain a profusion of stone, in the form of fountains, sculptures, patios, urns, balustrades and walls. During the Sung dynasty (AD 960–1279) the Chinese began to create miniature urban gardens, as described in Chapter 1. Their particular fondness was for water-washed rocks, colourful stones which arose from aeons of sedimentary deposits, pitted and shaped by the constant action of water. These rocks were highly sought after and proudly displayed in gardens as symbols of the great antiquity of the Chinese landscape. I share this liking, and at low tide scour the bed of the river Severn to bring back samples of river stone. Its delicate blue and slate-grey tones exactly match the colouring of the surface of the water when it reflects the reds and blues of a clouded evening sky.

The landscape gardens of eighteenth-century England often boasted a stone obelisk. This was believed to be a classical allusion, dating back to the days of the early pharaohs. But it would be necessary to travel further back than this to find the origin of standing stones, which played a central role in the religious ceremonies of Neolithic people. Rocks have always been objects of reverence and awe. The Israelites built a cairn of stones to mark their crossing of the river Jordan. Ayers Rock was the holy place of the Aborigines. In Jerusalem, the Dome of the Rock is built upon a massive outcrop of rock which was once used as an altar for burnt offerings. The stone bears cup marks, which suggests it was probably used for blood sacrifices in Paleolithic times. Muslims, when they make their pilgrimage to Mecca, travel round the holy stone of Maqam Ibrahim, so called because it is believed to bear the imprint of Abraham's foot. And today, when American tourists drive down Interstate 95 to see where the Pilgrim Fathers landed, their first stop is invariably Plymouth Rock, the historic stone on to which the new arrivals stepped when they left the *Mayflower* and first set foot in the New World. While rocks like these have become hallowed monuments, others have merely been called into temporary use as props in pagan rites. Stones have been beaten with hazel rods to induce rain. Women have sat in the hollows of stones to cure their barrenness. Country folk have walked three times round a monolith to ensure a good harvest and engaged couples have plighted their troth by clasping their hands through holes carved through stones. These customs have been observed for many millennia, and have not been expunged from the collective unconscious by our industrial culture.

With all this weight of history, stone – whether natural or reconstituted – makes a profoundly satisfying feature in a modern landscape garden. An upright stone in a garden acts as a symbol of energy and power, and it is no coincidence that the Greek deity Priapus was originally the god of both gardens and male potency. When we look at a stone we should be aware that it is not inert, but pulsating with atomic energy. We may laugh at those ancient legends which give upright stones the power to dance – like the Rollright Stones in Oxfordshire which are said to cavort at midnight on certain saints' days – but the truth is that the particles in even the most mundane stones are constantly vibrating to the endless dance of life. When we erect an obelisk or standing stone in a garden, we evoke some of the mystery and power of paganism. One of the most successful film series of all times is the *Star Wars* sequence. What is the reason for these films' universal popularity? At a superficial level they appear to be no more than typical science fiction fantasies, involved with unknown galaxies and interplanetary raiders. But deep down they awaken a powerful folk memory, for they have their roots in the ancient belief that life is pervaded by a universal energy which George Lucas, the films' writer/director, chose to call 'the Force'. The films caused such a frenzy, and developed such a cult following, that leading figures in Hollywood suggested that they should be made the focus of a new religion, based on the philosophical concept of the Force. This proposal was not pursued and in fact was quite unnecessary, for such an elemental belief has been a part of paganism since time began.

A BURNING QUESTION

ONE OF THE ESSENTIAL INGREDIENTS OF THE OLD RELIGION OF paganism was fire, probably the most potent and thrilling of the four Greek elements. Fire was vitally important to primeval man, who believed it to be the gift of the gods. According to the Greek myth, Prometheus brought that gift to earth and was punished for his audacity by being chained to a rock where his liver was constantly devoured by eagles. The arrival of fire was the first step on the path to civilization. Instead of spending their days gathering fruits and nuts, people could now hunt wild animals and cook them over an open fire, which preserved the meat for several days. The need to work together in hunting packs encouraged the development of co-operative behaviour and a sophisticated language system. Time could now be spent around the campfire, which became the centre of social life. Bonfires were lit for ceremonial purposes, generally as an act of worship to the sun god. Many hills in Britain have place names with the prefix or suffix 'Bell'. These were almost certainly sites where beacons were lit in honour of the sun god Bel or Baal. These rituals may no longer be observed, and yet gardeners still derive enormous, primeval pleasure from lighting bonfires or preparing barbecues, which re-enact elements of this pagan heritage.

When I look back on my childhood, two of my most vivid olfactory memories are of the smell of garden bonfires and the pungent aroma of smouldering campfires lit to celebrate the end of each day at schoolboy holiday camps. As a child, one of my greatest joys was lighting a fire on a river bank or in a wood-land clearing, using kindling scavenged from twigs, old birds' nests and scraps of bark from silver birch trees. While communal bonfires may be rare events today, the lure of fire remains. The open log fire still has a tremendous emotional appeal, despite the advent of central heating. We continue to light candles in memory of the dead, and an eternal flame burns over the tomb of the unknown warrior. To retain our links with this potent symbol of pagan power, we need to find time and space for bonfires, barbecues and candle-lit suppers in the garden.

THE WELL-ORIENTATED PERSON

THE IDEAL SOUL GARDEN SHOULD ACT AS A LIVING EMBLEM OF holistic integration, drawing together all its disparate elements. To serve this purpose it must have an overall configuration or gestalt, so that the whole becomes far greater than the compo-nent parts. Cosmologists may talk about generating an all-embracing 'theory of everything', but in practice we live in an atomistic age where objects and individuals tend to be viewed in isolation, and in microscopic detail. A holistic approach to gardening encourages us to take the opposite view. It draws our attention to the whole panorama of nature, rather than to a haphazard collection of rockery plants, cold frames and potting sheds. It acts as a telescope, through which our view is led outwards to the splendour and majesty of the entire universe.

A garden most readily achieves this end when it has a theme and a definite orientation. Sir Harold Nicolson, who designed the splendid garden at Sissinghurst, Kent, was convinced that gardens should have a coherent structure, with a main axis or backbone from which the other parts would hang. This axis 'should be indicated, and indeed emphasised'. My personal belief is that gardens, wherever possible, should bear a clearly defined magnetic orientation. Most animals have a homing instinct, which seems to be connected to their ability to orientate themselves in accordance with the earth's magnetic field. Tests carried out by geobiologist Professor Joseph Kirschvink, of the California Institute of Technology, have shown that the rainbow trout is able to 'smell' the difference between north and south. In its snout there are nerve endings which relay messages to the brain whenever a magnetic field is crossed. Dr Kirschvink says he would be 'totally surprised if we humans had lost this sense completely'. Subsequent tests have supported his belief, and suggest that we are born with powers of magnetic navigation but do not develop this innate ability to the same extent as homing pigeons and spawning salmon because we fail to put it to regular use. In addition, since we are now so often surrounded by artificially generated magnetic fields – created by computers, mobile phones, personal stereos and electric pylons – it is possible that this also confounds our in-built homing instinct. The likelihood is that the cells responsible for detecting changes in the earth's magnetic field are located in the human nose and sinus bones. If this is true, it gives new relevance to the old instruction 'follow your nose'!

When primitive man constructed his buildings and stone circles he made sure that they were correctly aligned. Most buildings were placed so that they faced towards the Orient, from which we derive the word 'orientation'. Christian churches have always been built so that worshippers sitting in the nave face directly east, towards the altar and the main east window through which the morning light shines. This was also the direction the Buddha faced when he found enlightenment sitting under the Bodhi tree. In the past, people of many races were buried with their feet facing east, and Elizabethan theatres were constructed so that their stages faced the same way. This orientation is also observed in China, where practitioners of *feng shui* insist that family life is enhanced whenever buildings face east.

In a world of constant flux it is good to be reminded that there are certain things which never change, like the direction of magnetic north. This discovery was one of the determining influences of Albert Einstein's life, a revelation which came when he was four years old and confined to bed with a mysterious illness. His father gave him a compass to play with. It was Albert's first introduction to the wonders of the universe. He marvelled at the constant alignment of the compass needle and the discovery made a lasting impression, helping to shape both his outlook and his later scientific development.

However much our personal lives may change, the world of nature remains invariable. A well-aligned garden fixed upon a consistent axis can help to remind us of this. The garden I am currently constructing faces south-east, but it has three standing stones set in a line which points due east. Here I plan to stand and watch the dawn rise, just to get my bearings. As I do so I will try to set my body to the cosmic clock and natural pace of life. At one time I shared the contemporary obsession with speed. When I set out on a country walk I tried to keep up a hectic pace of four to five miles per hour, even over rough or uphill ground. Now I realize that speed is purely relative. In future, when I rise at dawn and stand facing east in a contemplative frame of mind, I shall tell myself that I am not in fact standing still, but am supported on a globe which is hurtling through space at a speed of several hundred miles an hour. That surely is haste enough, a natural progression which occurs without any effort on our part.

When we meditate in this way, within natural surroundings, we realize that although we are discrete organisms, we are tied by invisible threads to everything else in the universe. This is the *nexus rerum* of the Greek philosophers, the web which connects all things. We are just spiders standing at the heart of a gigantic web which stretches out to every corner of the globe. When the early seafarers drew their navigational maps they invariably placed their own countries at the very centre of the chart. Their homeland was the hub from which the sea routes diverged like spokes from a wheel. As a result, when they were far away in unknown territory, they felt secure because they cherished the fond belief that whatever route they took would inevitably lead them home. The Chinese upheld this notion and named their country China or *chung-guo*, which means 'middle kingdom'.

One of the major tools of the *feng shui* expert is a special compass or *lo'pan*, which has a number of concentric rings. Each ring is filled with symbols which are a physical represent-ation of the cosmos and depict the carefully balanced relationship between the opposing forces of yin and yang. In the middle of this geomancer's compass is the symbol for the Heaven Pool, which represents the centre of the universe and the starting point for the radiation of the life force or *chi*.

In many ancient European cities it was a common practice to erect a large stone in the heart of the metropolis. This monolith marked the centre of the world and was called an 'omphalos', or 'navel of the world'. Our homes and gardens, however small, could well become the central points of our personal universes. I toyed with the idea of erecting a large omphalos in the middle of our garden as a constant reminder of this fact. Instead I have chosen a less conspicuous aide-mémoire. In a large paving stone in the centre of the garden I have chiselled a lemniscate, the horizontal figure-of-eight symbol which mathematicians employ to represent infinity. If I stand on this focal point and draw a line to the uttermost limits of the universe, the distances are exactly the same in all four directions. Whether I choose to move to the furthest point east, west, north or south the distances are always the same, always infinite – and so this spot must mark the centre of the universe. This ingenious argument, developed many centuries ago by a cosmologist with a pragmatic approach to life, was temporarily shattered by the discoveries of Copernicus, who revealed that the puny world we inhabit is just an obscure star in a minor galaxy. But the recent theories of quantum physicists have changed our viewpoint once again. They have shown that our previous concepts of position and separateness have little real meaning, for the waves the scientists observe are spread throughout all time and space in such a way that there is no distance between them and also no separateness. This conception, so different from the teaching of Descartes, Newton and Copernicus, has been summarized by David Bohm, one of the pioneers of quantum physics, as 'undivided wholeness'. Gardeners can easily accept such an idea, for it pictures an existence where we stand at the nebulous heart of an undifferentiated, holistic world which has no beginning and no end.

If we feel lost – emotionally or territorially – we need to re-discover where we stand. To enhance our knowledge of place, we have invented a system of lines of latitude and longitude which reveal where we are in relation to the equator and the international date line. These parameters were not available to our forebears, who lined themselves up with the sun and stars and prominent topographical landmarks. Many ancient buildings, cairns, camps, barrows, shrines and holy wells seem to have been aligned according to some preordained plan. Straight lines can sometimes be drawn to connect a number of these early pagan sites. Some investigators believe that prehistoric man had a keen sense of magnetic power and chose to build along these 'ley lines' because it was here that he was best able to tap the flowing energy of the earth. As one ley-hunter puts it, 'All the evidence from the remote past points to the inescapable conclusion that the earth's natural magnetism was not only known to men some thousands of years ago, but it provided them with a source of energy and inspiration to which their whole civilization was tuned.' The Chinese recognized remarkably similar topographical lines, known as *lung mei* or dragon paths. Whether or not these ley lines and *lung mei* exist, the concepts certainly suggest that we have an innate need to position ourselves within the vast universe of which we are but an infinitesimal part. A well-orientated garden can give us this feeling of grounding and connectedness. This may not be a matter of earth magic, as the geomancers suggest, but it can be exceedingly powerful psychological therapy in the Jungian sense: when we are grounded in time and space, and lose our feeling of loneliness and separation, we draw confidence and psychic strength from the awareness that we are at one with the world order and world mind, or collective unconscious.

Pope Gregory the Great was very scathing of the pagan British ways. At the start of the first century AD he observed: 'The English nation, placed in an obscure corner of the world, has hitherto been wholly taken up with the adoration of wood and stones.' He and countless other religious leaders tried to quell this earthy passion. A thousand years later King Knut attempted to stamp out the barbarous 'worship of stone, trees, fountains and heavenly bodies'. He too failed. Our pagan heritage persists, barely covered by centuries of religious and scientific acculturation. If our gardens are to perform their healing magic they must be places where we can commune with earth, stones, water and fire as readily as we now converse with solicitors, accountants, bank managers and tax inspectors.

A garden needs more than growing plants and a carefully manicured lawn if it is to create the illusion of a miniature wilderness. To make it a microcosm of the natural world it should include non-organic elements such as water, wood or stone. Water suggests fluidity, while wood and stone lend solidity and strength.

The Romans had a custom of placing a pebble in an urn at the end of each day, using a white pebble to mark a happy day and a black pebble for a less fortunate one. After thirty days they would empty the urn to review the month's events. We might consider copying this idea; a pottery cornucopia lying on its side and spilling forth a cascade of white pebbles would act as a permanent reminder of our good fortune.

Features which provide a sense of time and space, such as sundials and wind vanes, help to bring to a Soul Garden a feeling of permanence, rootedness and primeval strength. In this way it conveys the empowering message that we are not weak and isolated individuals but an integral part of an enduring cosmic whole.

CHAPTER FOUR

The Tree of Life

'And the leaves of the tree were
for the healing of the nations.'

THE REVELATION OF ST JOHN XXII, 2

*T*HERE WAS A TIME WHEN MEN WORSHIPPED TREES. VOTIVE offerings were hung on their branches, a custom which remains with us today in the tying of yellow ribbons of remembrance and the annual dressing of Christmas trees. At the end of the winter, pagan people joined hands and danced in circles around trees to welcome the arrival of the first leaf buds, a fertility rite still performed in some parts of England in the springtime, when schoolchildren dance around gaily decorated maypoles on the village green.

Trees were revered because they were the tallest and most enduring of all living organisms. In the mythology of the Native Americans the soul of the universe was thought to reside in a venerable, many-branching tree, the World Ash. But there were other, more practical reasons for holding trees in high esteem. The history of early human civilizations is in some ways the story of man's developing reliance on trees. Trees provided our hunter-gatherer ancestors with their daily nourishment of fruit and nuts. They built their homes with logs and made fires by rubbing one piece of wood against another. Some dispensed with artificial houses altogether and took shelter in the hollows of trees. This practice was so common in Malaysia that even today in Singapore the word *rukula* means both 'hollow tree' and 'house'. Many early races made their clothing from leaves and bark. Medicines were distilled from plants and trees. Aspirin came from the bark of the willow and quinine from the evergreen cinchona tree. So close was this link that the word for tree among many Bantu tribes is exactly the same as the word for medicine. Some of the earliest books were written on the inner layers of bark, a substance known in Latin as *liber*, which explains the derivation of our word 'library'. Hollowed treetrunks, covered with a leather flap, formed the earliest storage boxes, hence the term 'trunk' for a travelling chest. Some races hung their dead comrades on the branches of trees so that their bodies were raised closer to heaven, and would be eaten by birds rather than worms. Others buried their dead in hollow trees, which may explain our continuing preference for coffins made from wood rather than cheaper modern materials such as plastic and polystyrene.

Simple canoes were made from hollowed trees, and more sophisticated craft from worked planks of wood. Two thousand mature oak trees were required to make an eighteenth-century Royal Navy warship. This caused such a shortage of timber in Britain that a close friend and colleague of Admiral Nelson travelled the land with a pocket filled with acorns, which he stealthily planted in the gardens of his friends. With the coming of the Industrial Revolution wood was used increasingly as a fuel, to power the new glass factories and smelting works, and the greater its scarcity, the more costly it became, which gave landowners an added incentive to fell their forests. Trees were victims of their own versatility, a fate from which they couldn't escape until alternative sources of energy were found.

Parks and gardens filled with trees are valuable because they help to honour this ancient alliance between man and trees. Annual flowers are lovely but ephemeral; whenever we see them they remind us of the transience of life. But when we look at an ancient oak or yew we are confronted with the solidity, strength and permanence of nature. 'Every old tree of any sort inspires a beholder with a mystic feeling which leads him to a faraway world of timeless eternity,' wrote D. T. Suzuki in *Zen and*

Japanese Culture. Whatever the scale of our Soul Garden, that is the feeling which we should aim to create.

LIFE SUPPORT

TREES ENRICH OUR LIVES IN MYRIAD WAYS. THEY PROVIDE US with shade in the summer and shelter in the winter. They help to muffle city noise and soften or conceal the eyesores on the urban landscape, while in the countryside they safeguard the land from soil erosion. Fertile farmland can quickly be turned into arid dust bowls if it is stripped of the protection of hedgerows and woods, a disaster which befell the American prairies in the 1930s. We need the root structure of trees to bind the soil and provide a yearly carpet of falling leaves to feed the earth. Pollen records reveal that four thousand years ago the Peruvians denuded their land by deforestation and over-farming to such an extent that they were forced to migrate north. Here they planted trees to halt the erosion of the soil, and constructed highland terraces and stone irrigation channels, which produced an ideal agricultural economy. The prosperous land which resulted was called the 'navel of the Earth'. It was a model for other nations, until the Spanish conquistadores wrecked it by felling the trees to satisfy their demand for firewood, timber and fuel for smelting. Yet in spite of such warnings we are still denuding our farmland of trees for short-term commercial gain. As a result of this uncontrolled deforestation, the World Resource Institute estimates that since the end of the Second World War the planet has lost 10 per cent of its fertile soil – a vast tract of land, equivalent to the area of China and India combined.

Today we are desperately trying to find ways to reduce the atmospheric pollution of our cities. In the course of this quest we often overlook the enormous contribution that trees make towards the cleaning and refreshing of our urban air. During a year a single mature birch tree will filter tons of dust and diesel fumes and return them harmlessly to the ground in the autumn when its leaves fall. Every day a single tree will remove carbon dioxide from the atmosphere and generate enough clean oxygen to supply the lungs of ten people. What mechanical filtration system could be devised to match the elegance and cost-efficiency of this natural air-conditioning unit?

Trees also play a vital role in the rain cycle, keeping the earth's moisture in constant circulation. A mature poplar tree will absorb more than one hundred gallons of water a day from the soil, and then release it into the air by the slow and steady transpiration of its leaves. Those same leaves also function as food factories, producing the basic sugars upon which all plant and animal life depends. Each leaf contains a profusion of small, button-shaped cells known as chloroplasts, which store the vital green pigment chlorophyll. This is the magic catalyst for photo-synthesis, the process which uses the trapped energy of the sun's rays to turn supplies of carbon, hydrogen and oxygen into molecules of sugar. Photosynthesis provides all living animals with food to eat and oxygen to breathe. Without the constant sugar production of trees and shrubs and myriad blades of grass we couldn't survive.

The carbon dioxide content of the atmosphere has increased by a third since the start of the Industrial Revolution. Ecologists fear that this is creating a greenhouse effect which must inevitably lead to intolerable global warming. But their calculations do not allow for the protective function of trees. They do not take into account the fact that carbon dioxide stimulates tree growth. Tests carried out in Texas suggest that the likely increase in the atmospheric levels of carbon dioxide during the twenty-first century will double the number of trees and plants that survive. As a result it is predicted that a third of America's open deserts may soon be covered by forests.

TREE SURGERY

NOWADAYS IT IS OFTEN DIFFICULT TO ESCAPE THE SOUND OF chainsaws, as trees are felled to make way for new super-highways, or to produce the reams of paper needed to package our goods and to satisfy the voracious appetites of our computer printers and newspaper presses. This indiscriminate felling must be halted – in both urban and rural areas – or future generations will be left with lands stripped of fertility, bare of beauty and devoid of charm. This arboricide would have been totally abhorrent to devotees of the old pagan religions, who regarded trees as fellow spirits with feelings just like theirs. They believed that trees groaned with pain whenever they were damaged or killed, and their inhabiting spirits – dryads and nymphs – expelled. An old Greek legend tells of the fate of the vainglorious Erysichthon, who felled a sacred oak and was punished by the gods by being made to feel insatiably hungry for the remainder of his days. People brought up on these myths did not need to be urged to protect the rainforests; they cherished trees, without the compunction of Tree Preservation Orders. An old Wintu Indian found it difficult to comprehend the white man's desecration of his tribal lands in California. 'We don't chop down trees,' he said. 'We use only dead wood. But the white people plough up the ground, pull up the trees, kill everything. The tree says, "Don't. I am sore. Don't hurt me." But they chop it down and cut it up. The spirit of the land hates them.'

Despite our growing alienation from the natural world, we still maintain a pagan feeling of kinship with trees. Some Hindu men marry trees as a way of courting good fortune. (They believe it is lucky to marry three times, and if they cannot afford to support three wives they resort to the cheaper alternative of marrying one or two trees.) St Francis of Assisi spoke to trees. Rousseau drew strength from trees and wrote in his *Confessions*: 'When you see me at the point of death, carry me into the shade of an oak, and I promise you I shall recover.' Bismarck, the great Prussian statesman, used trees to help him relax. Whenever he was under stress he threw his arms around the nearest tree. Tree hugging is now a popular New Age cult, sometimes called the Chipko movement (the word *chipko*, from an Indian language, means 'to hug' – people hugged trees to save them from the axe). Others have reverted to the old practice of holding conversations with trees. Some people think this odd. You are thought holy when you talk to God, but insane if you talk to trees. Nevertheless some people regard trees as God's emissaries on earth, and choose to bare their souls to a tree rather than to a psychiatrist or father confessor. I respect that belief, and occasionally give a few words of encouragement to my favourite trees. But it's not necessary to go that far. It's possible to enjoy the therapy of trees without worshipping them, hugging them, talking to them, marrying them, dancing round them or decking them with gifts and decorative ribbons.

Whenever space permits, a garden should include a feature tree – an ornamental pear, for instance, or a weeping cherry – under which one can sit and contemplate the great unknown. This is a splendid exercise in relaxation, as was proved when brain wave studies were done of people looking either at trees or at houses and streets. The results showed that gazing at greenery produces a rise in alpha wave activity, which indicates an increased state of mental relaxation. This can benefit patients recovering from surgery, as was demonstrated by a study of twenty-three pairs of patients undergoing gall-bladder operations at a Pennsylvania hospital. All the patients received exactly the same post-operative care, and were housed in identical rooms except that one member of each pair looked out on a bare brick wall, while the other had the benefit of looking at trees in full leaf. The results showed that the patients who were able to view the trees made a better recovery than those who faced the bleak brick wall. They spent on average one day less in hospital, needed fewer than half the number of pain-killing injections and made a quarter as many complaints to the nursing staff.

The preservation and planting of trees is one of the first steps in the creation of a landscape garden, for practical as well as aesthetic reasons. Prince Charles bought Highgrove House, his country home in Gloucestershire, partly on impulse, because it had a splendid cedar tree standing on the west side of the house. 'I developed an instant passion' for the 200-year-old tree, he said. His first step in the construction of the Highgrove garden was to build a screen of yew trees around its perimeter, to give him added privacy and to provide a shelter from the keen winds which blow across the 500-foot-high Tetbury plain. Next he set about planting some of the feature trees which he had been given as wedding presents, which included tulip trees, a Boscobel oak and a pair of black mulberry trees. To ensure that these were properly placed, the Prince stood on the doorstep of the house using a megaphone, like an old-style movie director, to give instructions to his planting team. He then created a copse of sycamore, cherry, holly and ash trees. Most of these he planted himself, which has given him a paternal interest in their progress. 'They become remarkably like children whom you watch growing year by year,' he writes.

THE ASPEN'S SONG

THERE ARE FEW SOUNDS MORE SOOTHING THAN THE RUSTLING OF leaves. This was the first music to be heard on earth. According to the early Greek philosophers the melody of the spheres was created by the murmuring of the leaves of the Celestial Tree. Every one of the one hundred thousand types of tree on the planet sings its own song. I enjoy the sound of a rustling aspen, the one tree I can identify by ear alone. I stand in awe of those nature lovers who claim, as Thomas Hardy did, to be able to identify trees by the sound of their leaves. As Hardy wrote in *Under the Greenwood Tree*: 'To dwellers in a wood almost every species of tree has its voice as well as its feature. At the passing of the breeze the fir trees sob and moan no less distinctly than they rock; the holly whistles as it battles with itself; the ash hisses amid its quiverings; the beech rustles while its flat boughs rise and fall. And winter, which modifies the note of such trees as shed their leaves, does not destroy its individuality.'

PAUSE FOR THOUGHT

TREES, AS WELL AS GIVING DELIGHT TO THE EYE AND EAR, CAN ALSO be a source of spiritual inspiration. Buddha found enlighten- ment while he was sitting under a Bodhi tree. The early Jews studied their *krishma*, or office of daily prayer, while sitting under a fig tree, a practice commended by the Talmud. One sect of monks, which came to be known as the dendrites, spent their days meditating in the branches of trees. The Celts worshipped in sacred groves, which later became the site of Christian churches. Many of these are decorated with carved foliate heads, the symbols and relics of the ancient Celtic tree worship. (The word 'Druid' means 'knowing the oak tree', the oak being an object of worship as sacred to Druids as the cow is to a modern Hindu.)

If we spend only a few minutes a day sitting quietly under a tree, we will find it easier to lose our 'hurry sickness' and imbibe a sense of timelessness. These are precious, transcendental moments, which crowd eternity into an hour or stretch an hour into a lifetime. The historian Edward Carpenter underwent a spiritual experience which helped him to understand and identify with the pagan worship of trees. In his scholarly work *The Origins of Pagan and Christian Beliefs* he tells how, while he was admiring a beech tree bare of leaves, he suddenly became aware 'of its skyward-reaching arms and upturned finger-tips, as if some vivid life (or electricity) was streaming through them far into the spaces of heaven, and of its roots plunging into the earth and drawing the same energies from below . . . in that moment the tree was no longer a separate or separable organism, but a vast being ramifying far into space, sharing and uniting the life of Earth and Sky, and full of a most amazing activity'. This is in accord with the teaching of *feng shui*, which recommends that gardens should be planted with trees with upward-reaching branches, since this stimulates the flow of *chi*. Whatever the reality of this assertion, it is certainly true that looking at the upward surge of trees creates a feeling of positive energy.

Every time we glance up at the branches of a tree we get a glimpse of the sky beyond, reminding us of the vastness of the universe. The sky is an important part of a Soul Garden, and one good reason for planting trees is that they lead the eyes upwards, inspiring feelings of reverence and awe. The designers of Europe's medieval cathedrals set out to evoke this response, building their naves with fan-vaulted ceilings to mimic the intertwined branches of arcades of overhanging trees, in a style which came to be known as arboreal gothic. Goethe applauded this lofty attempt to mimic nature, and urged architects to 'Multiply, pierce the huge walls which you are to raise against the sky so that they shall ascend, like sublime, over-spreading trees of God, whose thousand branches, millions of twigs and leaves . . . announce the beauty of the Lord, their master.'

Nowadays we take the opposite stance: we try to surpass, rather than emulate, nature. We dominate the horizon by building skyscrapers which would dwarf even the loftiest tree. In a Soul Garden, where trees reign supreme, we need to bring ourselves and the world around us into a more natural and realistic perspective.

PLANTING FOR TOMORROW

THERE IS NO BETTER WAY TO MAKE REPARATION FOR THE DAMAGE we have done to our environment than by planting trees. This is a sacramental gesture which shows our commitment to the future and to the continuation of life. As a young man, Jean Jacques Rousseau was sent to board for a while with a family who lived in a village on the outskirts of Geneva. One of his most vivid memories of that visit was of the day the family united to plant a walnut tree, which was strategically placed so that it would eventually give shade to a terrace adjoining the house. The event was treated as a major ceremony, with songs being sung as the work was carried out. Thereafter Jean Jacques acted as the tree's guardian, making sure that it was regularly watered until its roots were firmly established. Throughout his life he felt a special kinship with that tree. 'Though I have lost all hope of ever seeing it now,' he wrote years later, in his *Confessions*, 'I still long to do so, and were I ever to return to that dear village and find my walnut tree still alive, I should most probably water it with my tears.' Others return time and again to trees they have planted in their youth. In 1869 the graduates of Vassar College planted a tree to mark the successful completion of their studies. This started a delightful custom which has been repeated by every subsequent graduating class. Each tree bears a commemorative plaque, and the alumni return annually to take part in reunions which culminate in the rededication of the trees. What a difference it would make to the landscape if every school adopted the same tree-planting rite!

When we plant a tree, we plant for posterity. A tree is our

finest monument, even though it may not bear a memorial inscription. 'If I knew I was going to die tomorrow,' said Martin Luther King, 'I would still plant a tree today.' At the start of the new millennium we should badger our town planners to turn our city streets into tree-lined boulevards. For trees deaden traffic noise, they provide nesting places for birds, clean the city air of pollutant particles and suck up excess moisture from the ground, helping to keep basements dry. They also make streets more desirable to live in, according to London estate agents, who report that the valuation of houses in tree-lined streets is approximately 15 per cent higher than that of homes in nearby roads which have no trees.

People who live in flats need not deny themselves the company of trees, for there is always the possibility of informally adopting one growing in a nearby public space. They can act as its guardian, visiting it at regular intervals to watch its growth and make sure that it is not being neglected or vandalized. New York has half a million trees lining its streets. All are protected from unauthorized interference by city by-laws, but all would benefit from human care and friendship.

Another custom worth promoting is the practice of giving trees to friends as house-warming presents or gifts to celebrate family births and wedding anniversaries. My wife and I have also made a practice of planting fruit trees to commemorate the passing of our closest friends. Whenever we wander through the garden we remember those we have lost and are reminded that, though they are dead, the flowers and fruits of their lives live on.

Our aim in developing a Soul Garden is to root ourselves in the eternal present. Every minute within its ambit we should exercise our senses to the full. A garden is a place where we can recollect the past in tranquillity, enjoy the present and look forward to the future.

canopy

A garden without trees is as hard to envisage as an art gallery without pictures. Trees soften the landscape. They provide shade in the summer and protection during the winter. A screen of trees around the house can provide enough wind-shelter to reduce by a tenth the energy consumption in the home. Their canopy of leaves acts as a highly effective pollution filter, absorbing many of the major atmospheric pollutant gases, including carbon monoxide, nitrogen dioxide and sulphur dioxide. Research also reveals that we are happier and more relaxed when we are in leafy surroundings, which helps to explain why average house prices in North America are 5–18 per cent higher in tree-lined areas.

In Norway it is customary to plant a tree to celebrate the birth of a baby, an ancient rite which could be extended to mark other occasions – a family death, a golden wedding anniversary or the visit of an old schoolfriend. If every inhabitant on the planet planted a tree this year, we would have no need to worry about the decimation of the rainforests, for we would bequeath to future generations the priceless legacy of six billion new trees. We owe it to them, and also to ourselves, to fill our gardens with trees, even if they can be no larger than the dwarf varieties grown in pots. Trees are a vital feature of a Soul Garden because they encourage wildlife, fix the soil, promote photosynthesis, assist the purification of the air and act as natural aids to meditation and relaxation.

CHAPTER FIVE

A Holy Alliance

'The kiss of the sun for pardon,
The song of the birds for mirth,
One is nearer God's Heart in a garden
Than anywhere else on earth.'

DOROTHY GURNEY, 'GOD'S GARDEN'

*G*ARDENING IS A THERAPY NOT ONLY FOR THE BODY AND mind but also for the spirit. It is amid the natural surroundings of plants and trees, rather than in man-made temples and shrines, that many people have had their first glimpse of the divine. St Augustine of Hippo was converted in a garden. St Francis of Assisi loved wandering in gardens and was so convinced of their enlightening power that he instructed his followers to set aside a plot of land for the cultivation of flowers, so that all who saw them might remember 'the Eternal Sweetness'. Nowadays we give great thought to the nourishment of our bodies, but pay little heed to the nourishment of our souls. Yet the two are indivisible, and however wholesome our diets we will not know optimum health and happiness if our souls are starved. In a garden our spirits are free to soar because we draw spiritual sustenance from our surroundings. This source of strength is recognized in the Koran, where the poor are advised to sell their last loaves of bread to buy hyacinths, as beautiful blooms will feed their souls.

Spirituality comes readily in a garden without the need for intellectual study or theological speculation. One keen gardener relates how gardening has been a gift of life to him, bringing joy where previously hopelessness and despair had ruled. When working in his garden, far removed from the cares and distractions of everyday life, he gets the feeling that he is in a deep dialogue with an unseen and silent partner. As a result, he writes, 'I have come to know true inner peace.' The pursuit of spiritual enlightenment is often seen as something remote and other-worldly, fit only for exceptional beings. This is a mistake. True spiritual enlightenment is about becoming more natural, more real, more totally alive, more fully human. It is about discovering our true identities and our proper relationship with the world about us and all other sentient beings. When we achieve enlightenment we do not set ourselves apart from the world, but become more fully part of it. Health, wholeness and holiness: these three words may appear to have different meanings but they share the same etymological root. To be holy is not to lead a life of remote asceticism, but to be more fully integrated into the cosmic whole. That is the true peace.

At times gardening can be back-breaking work, but no effort is needed to experience these uplifting feelings. They arise spontaneously provided we are in a receptive frame of mind. The ancient Greek philosophers held that human beings achieve the highest experiences when they lift their minds above the petty concerns of daily life and open them to what is eternal and universal. We do not need to take part in ceremonies or religious rites. In a garden 'the One' is present in the singing of a thrush, the perfume of a rose and the delicate tracery of a butterfly's wing. These experiences bring us nearer to God, although not necessarily closer to organized religion.

The Greeks believed that it was impossible to comprehend the essence of God. All we can do in this world is witness his creation, which demonstrates his all-pervasive life force or *energeiai*. A Latin inscription on the tomb of Sir Christopher Wren in St Paul's Cathedral reminds visitors that, if they want to see a monument to the achievements of that great seventeenth-century architect, they need do no more than cast their eye around them. In a Soul Garden, all you need to do if you wish to see evidence of the Creator is to look around you and admire his work. When we are surrounded by lush growth, exuberant forms and vivid colour, our eyes are drawn to the gifts of nature rather than to the handiwork of man and we know we are in the presence of God.

In the past the poor gardened from sheer necessity. They fed themselves on home-grown potatoes and peas, and kept a house cow and a few chickens to provide milk and eggs. That need rarely exists today, when most of us in the West feed our bodies only too well. Instead, we lack spiritual nourishment. This is what we will find, in the future, in the Soul Garden. Our fore-fathers tilled the soil to satisfy their physical wants; our children will garden to meet their spiritual needs. In doing so they will be following the example of Epicurus, Goethe, Rousseau and Thoreau – great philosophers who were also ardent gardeners. They lived close to the earth because it was from the natural world that they received the inspiration and elation of the divine *energeiai*.

THE SACRED GROVE

MANY SEVENTEENTH-CENTURY GARDEN DESIGNERS SET ASIDE A wild, uncultivated patch of land to be used as a private place of prayer and meditation. It was called the *sacro busco* or 'sacred grove', in recognition of the ancient Celtic practice of worship-ping in cleared patches of forest. The stylized Zen gardens of the Japanese Buddhist monks served a similar purpose. Our ancestors regarded God as an ineffable Great Spirit, the universal life force which animates every bird, tree, flower and shrub. Today we find it difficult to accept this simple concept. We want to anthropomorphize the Supreme Life Force. Is he a man or a woman? Black or white? Does he speak to us through the Koran, the Upanishads or the New Testament? We trivialize God whenever we attempt to make him conform to these man-made images and contrived theologies, for the Supreme Creative Force is all these things and at the same time none of them and yet much more than all.

There are many definitions of spirituality. According to one source it is 'the experience of meaning in everyday life', while another suggests that it is the act of uniting our 'true selves with the great whole of all beings'. If we accept either of these defin-itions as a starting point, it becomes evident that feelings of spiritual purpose and cosmic unity are more likely to be found in a *sacro busco* than in Piccadilly Circus or Times Square. In order to bring our religion down to earth we need to create our own *sacro busco*, a peaceful spot in the garden which can be used as a place of regular contemplation. This could be a seat under a tree, a garden house or a secluded, hedge-lined arbour. We should try to set aside a few minutes every day for medi-tation. As we sit in our quiet haven we should leave behind our worldly cares and bring into play what St Augustine described as 'the intellective organ of the heart', that part of our being which is neither rational nor emotive, but which offers us a direct, intuitive appreciation of God. The more we use this retreat the more effective it will be, for the more strongly it will come to be associated in our minds with feelings of repose and peace. Just as our digestive juices start to flow the moment we approach an aroma-filled kitchen, so we will begin to relax the moment we approach our appointed *sacro busco*.

Icons have been described as pictures which provide a 'window into heaven'. If this is their prime function, then a Soul Garden should be designed to act as a living, horti-cultural icon. Ideally it should form a green telescope, open to the skies but enclosed within a leafy framework which directs the gaze and acts as a barrier to distractions. If conditions permit, the garden should not be flat but three-dimensional, with soaring vertical lines to lift the eyes and the spirit upwards. This elevation can be achieved by planting trees, trellises and archways festooned with roses, clematis and honeysuckle. When we are depressed we instinctively cast our eyes down, whereas when we are elated we look to the heavens. We are by nature optimists, and in good times and bad we prefer to take the upward view – a truth recognized by the Greeks, who coined the name *anthropos*, 'the upward looker', to describe the human animal.

The inclusion of symbols and mottoes within a garden can be an additional aid to inspiration. A garden could contain a mosaic depicting the Tai Ji Tu, for example. This is the emblem of the Taoists, a circle broken up into two interlocking black and white tadpoles to represent the Supreme Ultimate, the union of the opposing forces of yang and yin. Other evocative symbols are the ankh, the key-like cross which was the ancient Egyptian sign of life, and the lemniscate, the symbol of eternity which I have carved in stone in the centre of my garden (see p. 84). In eighteenth-century England mottoes were often dis-played in gardens for the educational uplift of both family and friends. Perhaps garden centres would like to revive this tradition in the new millennium? After all, sundials often carry inscriptions drawing attention to the fleeting nature of time, like this one from William Blake: 'The hours of folly are measur'd by the clock; but of wisdom, no clock can measure.'

If heaven means to be one with God, as Confucius claimed, then gardeners have the good fortune to be able to create their own heavens here on earth. In their alfresco chapels they can observe the true spirit of prayer, which is often described as a conversation between God and man. Many people remember God only when times are hard, when their prayers become an endless litany of personal problems, concerns and wants. But when we sow seeds, prune shrubs or spread compost, our work itself encourages us to find time to *listen* to God, which is the true purpose and secret strength of prayer. As Prince Charles puts it, 'My spiritual and physical life are completely entwined with the garden . . . It is here I do my worshipping.'

A SOURCE OF WONDER

MOST PEOPLE HAVE A SPIRITUAL SENSE, AN AWARENESS OF something which lies beyond the sphere of their immediate existence. They have an impression of holiness, which is associated with feelings of wonder, love and awe. As human beings we may feel a degree of pride when we consider the ingenuity of a computer or a jet aircraft, but we can feel nothing but humility when we consider the majesty of the universe or the exquisite beauty of a minute flower. If we look up at the Pole Star, we may pause just long enough to realize that, while we now measure our lives in nanoseconds, that heavenly body is so remote that it would take us seven hundred million years to reach it if we were travelling at the speed of the fastest express train. That surely puts our brief lives into true perspective.

Every time we step into a garden we have the opportunity to

experience something of this feeling of reverence, which Rudolph Otto, the German religious historian, describes as the *mysterium tremendum* or 'awe-inspiring mystery'. In a Soul Garden there is no difference between God and nature, between the Creator and his creation. A love of nature and the worship of God go hand in hand, which is why in Japan it is not at all unusual to find Buddhists kneeling in prayer when they visit a lovely garden. Our lives are impoverished nowadays not because we lack objects of wonder but because we lack the ability to wonder. But if we look around even the most modest garden with a perceptive eye we can see Blake's 'World in a grain of sand, / And a Heaven in a wild flower'. As Tertullian, the second-century theologian, wrote: 'If I give you a rose you won't doubt God any more.' All we need to receive this spiritual reassurance is time to stand and stare, with open hearts and receptive minds.

All the great religions share this same source of pagan inspiration. Shintoism may acknowledge the existence of many diverse gods or *kani* – in rocks, streams, mountains and oceans – but its core belief is that there is one universal spirit which permeates the entire world. Taoism similarly recognizes the One, the mysterious essence which energizes the whole universe. Its followers are urged to return to nature as their source of inspiration, and to follow a policy of *wu wei*, a style of behaviour which models itself on the non-striving, effortless spontaneity of nature.

We in the West are culturally conditioned to worship God in temples, chapels and synagogues. This inevitably erects a barrier between the different religious groups, for although people in a multi-racial society may share the same schools, libraries, sports stadiums and supermarkets, they attend different places of worship. In a garden, however, we all worship at the same shrine, whatever our colour or creed. The sun and the wind and the rain are not the possessions of any particular sect. They belong to us all. They are part of our shared heritage: as Shakespeare observed, 'One touch of Nature makes the whole world kin.'

In a garden we see God in the parts and also in the whole. A single fir cone or seed head can be a source of endless wonder. More than seven hundred years ago an Italian mathematician, Leonardo Fibonacci, made a remarkable discovery. He studied the structure of fir cones, seashells and sunflower heads and found that their layers always showed a simple arithmetical progression, in which the number of units in the third layer was always the sum of the units in the previous two rows. Thus it remains true today that the numbers of segments in successive layers of a fir cone are always arranged in the order 1, 2, 3, 5, 8, 13. This is known as the Fibonacci sequence. It's not necessary to travel abroad to see the wonders of the world – the Great Wall of China or the Taj Mahal – for there are marvels to be found in every city park and private garden.

The story is told of a little boy who asked his father and then his local priest if anyone had ever seen God. Both did their best to answer him, but their replies made little sense and left him more confused than before. So he posed the same question to his next-door neighbour, who spent a large part of his time tending his garden. The man replied: 'Sometimes I think I never see anything else.' This is the revelation we may hope for every time we enter a Soul Garden, providing we switch off our cerebral faculties and instead apply our imagination and intuition. We should view the garden not with the analytical eyes of a scientist but with the mystical vision of a poet. Then we shall find, like Elizabeth Barrett Browning, that 'Earth's crammed with heaven and every common bush afire with God'.

Most of the time we worry about ephemeral things. We are made anxious by what we read in the papers or see on TV news bulletins. We yearn for a bigger house, a new car, stylish clothes or antique furniture – but in a garden we learn that the truly important things in life, the air we breathe and the sun's rays, cannot be possessed in the way that we can own material goods. The workaday world presents us with hustle, uncertainty and endless change, whereas in a garden we rediscover the regularity, stability and permanence of nature. When we create a Soul Garden we not only *create a place* of worship, we also *perform an act* of worship. Gardeners don't need miracles in order to believe in God. In fact, it is the sheer absence of any unexpected reversals of the natural law which makes us aware of God's dominion and power. Indeed, some atheists argue that nature is so perfect and well regulated that they do not need to postulate the existence of a divine Creator. That must surely be the highest possible praise of God.

EXPERIENCING THE LIFE FORCE

CIVILIZED LIFE AS WE KNOW IT TODAY WOULD COME TO AN END IF we were deprived of man-made sources of power – electricity, petrol and gas. But a garden is driven by a totally different force, and the moment we step into one we should feel ourselves connected to this primordial source of energy. The ancients dubbed this universal life force the *anima mundi*, the Chinese called it *chi*, and the Hindus *prana*. This is the potent, imperceptible source of vitality, health and healing which we imbibe whenever we enter a Soul Garden.

The idea of gardening as a source of mystical communion with the great life force may sound fanciful or bizarre. But it was Albert Einstein, one of the greatest scientists of the twentieth century, who said: 'The most beautiful and most profound emotion we can experience is the sensation of the mystical. It is the sower of all true science.' Each of us has a capacity for mysticism. In order to awaken it, we need to make our gardens living temples, places to experience the intimate collaboration between God and man, where nature and artifice are seamlessly blended. In the West we tend to make a sharp distinction between our physical selves and the environment we inhabit, between self and non-self. This division is not nearly so clear in the Orient, and in fact until very recently the Japanese had no word for 'nature'. It was not until late in the nineteenth century that they coined the term *shizen* to describe the Western concept of nature as 'a world beyond ourselves'. Prior to that time they had always regarded mankind not as separate but as an integral part of the cosmos.

That sense of cosmic union is something which must be fostered within a Soul Garden. We can begin by contemplating a tree: with its roots firmly planted in the earth from which it draws its nourishment, the tree then sends its arms reaching upwards to the sky from where it absorbs the life force. The Japanese remind themselves of this in their ikebana flower arrangements, which portray a triangle in which the two lower angles represent the link between man and the earth, and the upward pointing angle the ascent into heaven. The heaven envisaged in these flower arrangements is not a place so much as a state of mind, an awareness that we are not isolated creatures but are at one with the rest of creation.

When we escape the rat race and enjoy a few moments' relaxation in a private *sacro busco*, our conception of time changes. It is as if one day becomes a thousand years, and a thousand years a single day. Our souls begin to see things as God sees them *sub specie eternitatis*, without beginning or end, whole and yet infinitely varied, forever changing and yet endlessly the same. To attain this state of mind we need to be totally, but effortlessly, absorbed in the sight and sounds and smells of our surroundings. It is this complete enthralment which is the essence of the mystical experience.

In this state of relaxed fascination we are able to absorb the many lessons that nature has to impart. Here we find Shakespeare's 'tongues in trees, books in the running brooks,/Sermons in stones, and good in everything'. From ants we learn the virtues of industry, from bees the rewards of co-operative behaviour and from birds the strengths and joys of freedom. Indeed, many people have derived uplift and comfort from watching the antics of birds. A woman named Pat Hartridge was seriously ill in Churchill Hospital, Oxford, struggling to overcome a bout of legionnaires' disease. Her spirits were at a very low ebb until she started to observe the perky behaviour of a robin which regularly perched on the sill of her hospital window. This bird, the epitome of natural vitality, gave her back the will to live. After her recovery she launched a scheme, in association with the Royal Society for Nature Conservancy, to encourage the creation of wildlife gardens within hospital grounds. Several of these have now been established and are bringing convalescent patients the healing benefits of the *vis medicatrix naturae*.

The book *Jonathan Livingston Seagull*, by Richard Bach, has also been a source of inspiration to many who have come to realize that there is more to life than mindless routine. Like the maverick seagull Jonathan Livingston we are not compelled to follow the flock but are free to strike out on our own. It is a simple but compelling allegory, and when the *British Medical Journal* polled its readers to select the book most likely to broaden the horizons of doctors and medical students, the one which came top of the list was *Jonathan Livingston Seagull*.

INTIMATIONS OF ETERNITY

THE SOUL GARDEN IS A HOTBED OF GROWTH, FOR PEOPLE AS well as for plants, for here we learn to be still, we lose our feelings of alienation and become one with the cosmic whole. Although cosmologists today are seeking a mathematical formula which will provide a Theory of Everything, it is important to remember that primitive man discovered that unifying principle a long while ago and called it the Supreme Ultimate or the Great Spirit. Instead of following a process of scientific deduction, our ancestors realized intuitively that there was a unity in all things. An anthropological study of the ancient religious beliefs of tribes in Australia, Africa, Asia, Siberia, New Guinea and North and South America, carried out in the early 1900s, showed that all the cultures examined, however diverse, believed that everything on earth – stones, rocks, trees, birds, streams and pools – was simply an individual reflection of the one cosmic soul.

'He who sees the Infinite in all things, sees God,' wrote William Blake. That is what we should aim to do in a Soul Garden. Scientists today are rediscovering this age-old concept. Chaos theorists assure us that we do not act in isolation. They talk of the Butterfly Effect, whereby the flap of a butterfly's wings in Nebraska can cause a typhoon in Taiwan. Mathematicians, working with computers, have developed the new science of fractal geometry which has revealed that even such diverse forms as mountains, clouds, snowflakes and plants share the same structural patterns. Researchers carrying out DNA studies have found exceedingly close genetic links between fruit flies, worms and man. These researches show that it is necessary to modify only 14 per cent of the nucleotides in a yeast organism to convert it into a human being. We have more in common than we could possibly imagine with the simplest of living creatures. It is a sobering thought.

Previous societies, which lived in far closer contact with nature than we do, had little need to be convinced of this essential truth. The Sioux Indians spoke of *wakonda*, a oneness with the universe. Hindus practised yoga, which means 'union' with the cosmic whole. This 'oneness' is also a key tenet of the Buddhist doctrine. In the words of the *Dhammapada Buddha*, 'There is no difference between the sun and man. There is no such thing as my body, or your body, except in words. It is all one. Sun, moon, mineral, man.' This is an exceedingly difficult concept for Westerners to embrace. Self-assertion is one of our primary motivations. Every time we write our CV we emphasize the unique qualities that make us superior to every other human being. We dress to assert our individuality, we battle for autonomy at work and we strive for the right to 'do our own thing' in our leisure hours. So it is not easy for us to embrace the idea that we have existential links with our next-door neighbour, let alone with the moon and stars. We could easily make the mistake of the well-intentioned noviciate who asked his Buddhist teacher what enlightened people could do to help the uninitiated. To which he got the reply: 'When you have achieved understanding, there are no other people.'

These are lessons we can gently assimilate in a Soul Garden. Within this environment we are able to focus less on the differences between things and instead come gradually to appreciate their similarities. Slowly we learn to eliminate the false dichotomies between animal and vegetable, plant and weed, living and dead. Gradually we blur the distinction between self and non-self. Without making any conscious effort, we come to recognize that we 'are bound up in the bundle of life'. Like drops of dew falling from a lotus leaf, we are carried away in the stream of life until we finally merge together in the one great cosmic pool. The lotus has its roots firmly planted in the earth but it is not a part of the mud, for it raises its stem through the water and lifts its petals to face the sun. Rooted in the soil but climbing towards the heavens, the lotus has become a universal symbol of transcendence and uncorrupted purity.

Those blissful moments when we feel at one with the whole of creation are rare and fleeting. They are often described as 'peak experiences' or, in the words of Romain Rolland, 'oceanic feelings'. Rolland wrote a challenging letter to his friend Sigmund Freud, saying that the founder of psychoanalysis didn't understand the true source of religious experience. These sentiments stemmed, said Rolland, 'from a "sensation of eternity", a feeling as of something limitless, unbounded – as it were "oceanic".' Freud was so impressed by the idea of oceanic feelings that he made the concept his own, without giving credit to his friend. These peak experiences cannot be forced but tend to sneak up on us unexpectedly, when we are watching the gentle movements of a stream, lying in a meadow looking up at the clouds on a bright summer's day or idly observing the butterflies as they flit from flower to flower in a wilderness garden. On a visit to England Carl Linnaeus, the great Swedish botanist, saw for the first time a gorse bush covered with yellow blooms. He was so entranced by its beauty that he fell to his knees and gave thanks to God. When Charles Darwin first caught sight of the Brazilian rainforest he was overcome by a feeling of 'wonder, astonishment and sublime devotion'. Our lives are ennobled by such experiences, for when we witness the marvel and majesty of the world about us, I believe we look into the face of God.

ALL GOD'S CREATURES

OUR SUCCESS AS SOUL GARDENERS DEPENDS, NOT ON THE NUMBER of rare plants we can cultivate, but on the number of our fellow creatures we can attract to share our private Shangri-Las. If we are to experience that oceanic feeling we must learn to befriend birds, butterflies, dragonflies, squirrels, hedgehogs and frogs. To make them welcome, we should grow berried trees and shrubs to encourage birds, dig ponds to attract frogs and toads, and leave piles of dead wood where field mice can make their homes. We should plant heathers and lavender to provide pollen for bees, and grow buddleias to give butterflies their essential breeding grounds. Our gardens must become private nature reserves where we treat even the lowliest creatures as our welcome and respected friends.

To do this may involve a major change in outlook. If we were raised within the Judaeo-Christian tradition, we were brought up to believe that God gave man dominion over every living creature that moves on the earth. Now we have to accept that we are all equal partners in the great cosmic plan. An earthworm is neither inferior nor superior to man, it is just far better equipped for living underground and serving its function as an unpaid tiller of the soil. We must abandon the idea of higher and lower animals, and the Darwinian concept that man is perched on a lofty throne at the top of the evolutionary tree.

As gardeners we are forced to face our limitations. We don't live as long as yew trees or breed as rapidly as ladybirds. We can't fly, we can't move as quickly as a rabbit, or jump like a toad. In fact if the Olympic games were open to all members of the animal kingdom we would not win a single event. Our only unique possession is our highly developed brain, and we use it to such singularly poor effect that we spend a large part of our lives fretting about our past and future problems. Animals, with their less highly developed imaginations, are untroubled by such concerns.

We can learn from animals, and we can also benefit from being in their company. One American journalist discovered for herself that animals can act as spiritual guides, showing us how to live in closer contact with the Spirit of the Universe. She was suffering from depression, which had been eased only briefly by a stay at an expensive addiction clinic in the Arizona desert. She decided to try a different kind of cure, at a small fishing village on the shores of the Red Sea, where she would be able to swim with dolphins. One dolphin immediately befriended her. His warm welcome 'touched me beyond words', she wrote. 'My sense of time and place faded completely. What seemed like a few minutes' swimming turned out to be an hour and a half. As I left the water . . . I suddenly felt full of joy, the tension left my body and a huge smile fixed on my face, I was "blissed out".'

We are renewed and restored by our contact with pets and garden animals. Research has revealed that, within a few moments of purchasing a cat or dog, people experience an immediate reduction in minor problems such as headaches, insomnia, backache, anxiety and fatigue. Studies carried out by Dr James Serpell of the Companion Animal Research Group at Cambridge University showed that, after a month, new pet owners show 'a quite amazing and instantaneous change in their health measures'. Another study of over five thousand patients attending the Baker Medical Research Institute in Prahran, Australia revealed that pet owners had lower than average cholesterol levels and blood pressure.

Many people are now keeping fish tanks in their homes and offices to help them relax. Desmond Morris, the world-famous zoologist, did so for many years and claims: 'Fish take you as far away from human concerns as you can get.' Tests show that watching the rhythmic movement of tropical fish in a tank produces a lowering of tension and blood pressure levels. Personally I have no doubt that the same relaxing effect could be obtained by feeding sparrows on a garden patio, or nurturing a row of broad beans.

In a garden we learn the first and most important principle of ecology, that everything is connected to everything else. People beset with mental problems often embark on long courses of self-examination, hoping to find an escape from their angst by exploring the world within. In the process they become increasingly self-absorbed and isolated from the world around them. The cultivation of a Soul Garden offers a more extrovert solution, for as we become more closely integrated with the world of nature, more aware of our place in the cosmic whole, we lose our sense of alienation, self-obsession and existential angst.

According to the Native Americans, when the Great Spirit formed the universe he created a triumphal song which was written in numerous parts. He gave one part to the trees and other parts to the earth, rocks, birds, animals and human beings. This hymn is complete only when the whole choir of nature sings in unison. A prime function of a Soul Garden is to help us forget our individual differences and lend our voice to swell that cosmic anthem.

All gardens represent a collaboration between God and man. This partnership should be particularly evident in a Soul Garden, which will be designed to act as an inspiration to worship. It should be a place of mystery, richness and overwhelming natural beauty, an environment which quickens the senses, where wildlife thrives and flowers and plants proliferate.

The effect of wonder and astonishment will be increased if our gardens are designed to reflect our personal conception of a small, self-contained paradise. Our working lives are fragmented, bedevilled by the state which psychologist William James described as Zerrissenheit *or 'torn-to-pieces-hood'. In a Soul Garden we should overcome this sense of fragmentation and cosmic alienation and be made to feel that we are entering a* sacro busco, *a quiet, unspoilt place where we can transcend the concerns and distractions of our individual daily lives and achieve a closer union with the universal whole.*

CHAPTER SIX

A Beauty Spot

'He who would have beautiful roses in his garden must have beautiful roses in his heart.'

DEAN SAMUEL HOLE, 1869

*T*HE GREAT DANGER OF LIVING IN A MODERN CITY IS NOT THAT we will be deafened by noise or killed by exhaust fumes, but that we will be starved of natural beauty. We desperately need to bring beauty into our lives. We take pains to make ourselves look as attractive as possible, but as a generation we make remarkably little effort to enhance the appearance of our surroundings. This is a mistake, as recent medical research shows that our sense of well-being is closely related to the visual qualities of our environment.

In 1956 Abraham Maslow, one of the pioneers of humanist psychology, carried out some telling experiments to determine the effect of attractive surroundings on human performance. He enlisted the help of a team of examiners, who asked a group of forty-two students to look at a set of portrait photographs to determine whether the subjects were irritable or contented, tired or energetic. The students were shown these photographs twice, once when they themselves were sitting in a beautiful room with attractive furniture, nicely painted walls and pleasing lighting, and again when they were seated in a drab, dirty room filled with litter. The results showed that their assessments of the subjects' energy levels and well-being were significantly higher when they were working in the aesthetically attractive setting. But there was a hidden twist to these experiments, for Maslow was secretly recording the behavioural responses of the examiners as well as the students. These covert observations revealed that throughout the three-day experiment the examiners showed high levels of comfort, energy and enjoyment when they were working in the attractive room, but revealed evidence of increased irritability, discontent and tiredness when they carried out the same tasks in the unsightly setting.

We feel better, it seems, when we are in a beautiful environment. But what is the secret of beauty's healing power? The eighteenth-century German philosopher Friedrich Schiller pondered this question in his book *Lessons on the Aesthetic Education of Man*. The conclusion he came to was that beauty, whether in a painting, a piece of music or natural scenery, helps to fuse the two sides of human nature, the rational and the emotional. 'Only the perception of the beautiful makes something whole of man, because both of his natures accord with it,' he wrote. Nietzsche came to a similar conclusion. He described the two sides of human nature as the Apollonian and the Dionysian, after the two Greek gods, Apollo, the god of order and reason, and Dionysus, the god of emotion and passion. 'Art approaches us as a redeeming and healing enchantress,' said Nietzsche. The healing comes because beauty brings about a fusion between the rationality and order of Apollo and the fervour and abandon of Dionysus.

The early Christian saints held that all forms of beauty are an expression of the divine. They argued that the world is naturally good and naturally beautiful because it is a manifestation of God's presence. According to this argument, evil and ugliness arise through man's intervention. We have been given the gift of free will, an endowment we frequently abuse. We make the wrong choices. We have the power to surround ourselves with things which are unsightly and stark, or to fill our lives with harmony and loveliness. Failure to choose what is beautiful is both a social and a moral offence, in the opinion of theologian Dean Inge, who wrote: 'If those philosophers are right who hold that beauty is an attribute of the Deity, and that ugliness of every kind is displeasing in His sight, our modern civilisation is a blatant blasphemy.' We may feel powerless to bring about any immediate improvements in the appearance of our towns and cities, but we can at least begin to make a difference in our own homes and gardens.

THE WONDERS OF THE WORLD

IT IS THROUGH NATURE THAT WE FIRST COME TO APPRECIATE beauty. Even children as young as four or five will comment spontaneously on the loveliness of natural scenery. In 1924 Edith Newcomb carried out a study of two thousand British and American schoolchildren aged between seven and thirteen. This study showed that youngsters of all ages are keenly aware of the beauty of nature. To begin with their taste is largely for bright colours and pretty flowers, but as they mature they begin to take delight in subjects such as sunsets, moonlight, rainbows, seascapes and spectacular scenery. One ten-year-old described a glorious sunset she had witnessed and said, 'Every day I long to see another sunset like this.' Others spoke of the pleasure they got from observing the graceful, drooping branches of willow trees, the delicate curve of a swan's neck or the intricate shapes of snowflakes under a magnifying glass.

Nature has always been a prime source of artistic inspiration. Leonardo da Vinci was an attentive student of nature, undertaking regular trips to the Vatican gardens to make detailed drawings of plants, flowers and trees. It is by observing nature, either in the wild or in a cultivated landscape, that we develop our aesthetic sense. In fact one of the criteria by which we may gauge the success of a Soul Garden is its ability to provide artistic inspiration and provoke aesthetic delight. As the art critic Herbert Read wrote, 'Immediate joy-in-perception is the final sanction of aesthetic experience.' A garden works when the sight of it evokes instantaneous pleasure.

When we visit a memorable garden such as Chatsworth, Stourhead or Sissinghurst, we almost always return home with a longing to do something to beautify our own garden plot. This happened to Charles VIII of France, who travelled to Italy in 1495 to seize the throne of Naples. He failed to capture the kingdom, but was himself captivated by the Neapolitan gardens. He wrote back to his cousin Pierre de Bourbon: 'You cannot believe what beautiful gardens I have seen in this town: for, on my word, it seems as though only Adam and Eve were wanting to make an earthly paradise, so full are they of rare and beautiful things.' Returning to France, he took with him a team of twenty-two artists whom he entrusted with the task of introducing the new Italianate style of house and garden design. This marked the start of the French Renaissance and paved the way for the creation of such splendid gardens as those of Villandry and Fontainebleau.

Garden books and magazines are a rich source of new ideas. Recently I spotted a newspaper picture of a tree encircled by mighty clumps of *Gunnera manicata*. This is an effect I would love to create in my garden, but would the plant thrive where I aim to put it, in the shade of a lofty cedar? There is only one way to find out – plant it and see. And that's how gardens evolve.

Through the creation of a lovely garden, however modest, we contribute to the evolution of a more beautiful landscape. Even the surroundings of a drab terraced house or flat can be transformed by the judicious use of window boxes, hanging baskets and trellis-grown climbing plants. City basements, so often allowed to become unsightly refuse dumps, can be made to look delightful if they are given a lick of paint and festooned with potted plants and climbing shrubs. Indeed, plants can be used like cosmetics, to accentuate attractive features and mask blemishes. When the view from a living-room window is of billboards, garages and parking lots, it can be softened by growing house plants on glass shelves placed *inside* the window. With supermarkets and garden centres now selling a wide range of indoor plants, it has never been easier to bring the beauty of the countryside into the home.

PICTURESQUE AND SUBLIME

OVER THE YEARS THERE HAVE BEEN MANY DIFFERENT interpretations of utopia, but every one has been conceived as a place of outstanding beauty, invariably filled with glorious gardens. Thomas More stressed in his *Utopia* that the inhabitants of Amaurote 'set great store by their gardens ... so pleasant, so well furnished and so finely kept'. Himself a passionate gardener, in 1520 he bought a plot of land in Chelsea, on the banks of the Thames, where he created a garden 'of marvellous beauty, full of lovely flowers and blossoming fruit trees'. In the years which followed, many English people emulated his example and tried to plant gardens which would act as private, earthly paradises. One of the first great books on garden design, written by John Parkinson in 1629, was in fact called *Paradisi in Sole Paradisus Terrestris*, 'an earthly paradise in a lonely garden'. A century later the aesthetic movement gave a further boost to landscape gardening. Many people read Edmund Burke's book *Philosophical Inquiry into the Origin of our Ideas on the Sublime and Beautiful*, published in 1756, and immediately set out to create gardens which were objects of beauty rather than flamboyant displays of wealth or utilitarian allotments for growing vegetables and fruits. The greatest praise at that time was to create a garden which was judged to be 'sublime'.

The great garden designers of the eighteenth century, such as William Kent, looked to painters rather than philosophers for their inspiration, although the objective was still to strive for beauty rather than opulence or practicality. Gardens had to be 'picturesque'. Whatever the term used, the important thing was to capture the spirit of the Romantic movement and design gardens which were as moving as a nature poem by William Wordsworth and as pretty as a painting by Poussin. Nowadays it would cost a small fortune to buy a landscape painting by Constable, Claude or Corot, but we can create our own landscape in miniature for a fraction of the price. The natural sights, sounds and scents of a garden can never cloy, for the natural world is not static like a painting, but in a constant state of flux. While I write this book, I find myself gazing out through my study window. The view is never the same. It changes with the seasons, the cloud formations, the time of day, the rising of the wind and the arrival of the occasional shower of rain. For me, the view from my study is worth an entire art gallery of landscape paintings.

A ROMANTIC DREAM

GEORG HEGEL, THE GERMAN PHILOSOPHER, HELD THAT CERTAIN things in nature can be made more pleasing by astute rearrangement. The purpose of art, he claimed, was to bring about this aesthetic realignment. This is the prime object of garden design. A natural garden, like a landscape painting, is a carefully crafted artifice. It is man-made, and succeeds insofar as it achieves an artistic arrangement of a collection of natural elements in a way which masks all signs of human effort and creates an illusion of spontaneity.

A pedantic distinction is sometimes made between fine art and applied art. Music, poetry and painting are judged to be different, and in some way superior, to the applied arts such as pottery, weaving and basket making. This distinction is meaningless to an avid gardener, for gardening combines both the fine art of garden design and the ongoing applied art of garden development and maintenance. The person who gardens with their hands alone is a labourer. The person who works with their hands and head is a gardener; but the individual who brings to the garden their hands, head and heart is a true horticultural artist. Those rare people who labour *and* think *and* feel are the ones who create gardens which merit the description 'sublime'.

A useful starting point when designing a Soul Garden is to determine its overall theme. It should be conceived as a whole rather than a pastiche of unconnected fragments, and composed with the same skill as a well-designed painting, balancing colour, texture and form. There needs to be a unity in the design's complexity, whether the canvas is large or small. When

Frederick Olmstead designed Central Park, New York, he told the city commissioners: 'The Park throughout is a single work of art, namely that it shall be framed upon a single noble motive.' In his case the motive was to preserve the original landscape of Manhattan. This overriding objective dominated all his subsequent plans, and determined that in his use of the land he would 'interfere with its easy, undulating outlines, and picturesque, rocky scenery as little as possible'.

When the painter Claude Monet created his garden at Giverny, the focal point was its now famous lily pond. This he excavated by his own efforts. To keep it topped up with water he dug a channel linking it directly with the river Seine, an unauthorized act which angered his neighbours. Once the pond was full he planted it with water lilies. This inspired him to construct a Japanese bridge from which the lilies could be admired. To add an air of romance and mystery he surrounded the pond with wisteria, hollyhocks, gladioli and roses. Beginning with a central image, Monet's garden became a lifetime passion and his major source of artistic inspiration for the remainder of his life.

A Soul Garden needs a leitmotif, and although this will depend to some extent on the personality of the individual owner, it must be a theme which inspires feelings of beauty, restfulness, spirituality and close harmony with nature. This ambience is most easily conveyed in gardens which are romantic, wild, mysterious, unexpected and 'sublime'. As we saw in Chapter 3, straight lines are best avoided. In a Soul Garden the aim is to induce a mood of easy, relaxed sensuousness, an effect most easily achieved with muted tones and gentle undulations rather than jagged lines and jazzy colours.

GREEN THOUGHTS

THE USE OF COLOUR IN A GARDEN IS VERY MUCH A MATTER OF personal taste, and here I must expose my own preferences and prejudices, which I know do not meet with universal approval. Most garden books emphasize the importance of colour, talking in terms of blending vivid splashes of red geraniums with blue lobelias, or yellow broom with purple violas. These brilliant colours undoubtedly have their attractions, but to me they are more suitable for a Walt Disney cartoon than a wild, natural garden. Nature is full of colour – but the colour green, which dominates our landscape, is often overlooked. The term covers an infinite variety of shades, from mint green to lime, from pea green to apple and olive, all subtly evocative of nature's bounty. We should make better use of green.

Colours are the lingua franca of our subconscious minds and are known to have a profound effect on our behaviour. Red, for instance, is a recognized danger sign, universally employed in warning signals and traffic lights. When we are angry we are said to see red, and exposing the body to red light increases blood sugar levels, a change which also occurs when we are under stress. Red is also a sexual stimulant. It is the colour of the engorged male phallus, while the crimson rump of a female monkey in heat acts as a mounting signal for nearby males. Red is the traditional colour of lipsticks and rouge, chosen because it accentuates the facial flushing that women show when they are sexually aroused. Green, on the other hand, is a restful colour, a sign of safety. In the Islamic tradition it represents peace. Tests in psychology laboratories have shown that time is judged to move more slowly in a green room than in one which is painted red. Green is also the conventional colour of simplicity and lack of sophistication, which is why we call in-experienced people greenhorns.

There can be no doubt that colour affects our mood. A study of Canadian schoolchildren showed that pupils responded better when teachers corrected their exercise books with green ink markings and comments, rather than with the more customary red. 'Red is an aggressive colour,' explained a colour psychologist commenting on the experiment. 'On the other hand, green gives off a more relaxed message of harmony, balance and universal love.' This is the message that should be conveyed by a   . Gertrude Jekyll, who put her indelible stamp on English garden design in the early twentieth century, was always admonishing her followers: 'Remember green is a colour.' Green is the restful colour chosen for the walls of oper-ating theatres, and it should predominate in a healing garden. When we step into a harmonious world of subtle colour we should experience the feeling which Andrew Marvell captured so well in his seventeenth-century poem 'The Garden': 'Meanwhile the mind, from pleasures less,/Withdraws into its happiness . . ./To a green thought in a green shade.'

Colours should match our personality and mood. Garden centres may tempt us to stock our gardens with the very latest varieties of brightly coloured tulips or bedding plants, or offer us hybrid shrubs which give such a profusion of blooms that the flowers obscure the form and texture of the underlying plants. Personally, I am not drawn to such displays. I prefer to enliven my garden with a generous planting of evergreen shrubs – berberis, hebes, holly and laurels – which provide round-the-year colour and become especially romantic on a dull winter's day when their shiny leaves are glistening in the rain.

Evergreen trees as well as shrubs are a wonderful source of restful colour. When William of Orange came to the throne in 1689 he brought with him from Holland a particular fondness for trees which would retain their colour throughout the grey British winters. Some of these newly imported trees, such as the cedar of Lebanon, struggled to survive in the inclement northern climate, so they were raised and acclimatized under glass – and this is the origin of the word 'greenhouse'.

That love of evergreen shrubs remains today and with it a passion for emerald lawns. Over three hundred years ago Francis Bacon wrote: 'Nothing is more pleasant to the eye than green grass kept finely shorn.' Walt Whitman loved a well-kept lawn, which he described as 'the handkerchief of the Lord'. Even a single blade of grass gave him cause to reflect on the beauty and wonder of nature: 'I believe a leaf of grass is no less than the journey-work of the stars,' he wrote in 'Song of Myself'.

A rich green lawn, free of weeds and close cut to give that lovely striped effect, is indeed a thing of exquisite beauty. But it isn't easy to acquire, and lacks the naturalness and spontaneity of rough meadow grass. An American tourist greatly admired the lawns at Hampton Court and asked the head gardener for his secret. 'It's easy,' the gardener replied, 'just mow it twice a week for a thousand years.' This, in fact, was only a partial answer for an immaculate lawn requires regular weeding, feeding, rolling and scarifying. Whether we need such a high standard of perfection is a matter of choice, for surely it is more important for gardens to be places of leisure and pleasure than labour-intensive workshops.

The more time we spend in green and beautiful surroundings the more easily we may find inner harmony and peace. It might seem remarkable to claim that gardening can even bring about a change in moral outlook, but this was the firm belief of the early philosophers. Plato was convinced that the perception of beauty brought about an *anamnesis*, or remembrance, of all previous encounters with the beauty of the natural world. In this way beauty begets beauty, in a chain reaction which Plato believed spilled over into a passion for goodness and spiritual wisdom. We become better people through being in a beautiful garden, and the more time we spend within its bounds, the more we benefit from its healing and sustaining powers.

Landscape design is one of the oldest and most satisfying of all the decorative arts. It's an artistic skill that is urgently needed today to offset the bleak ugliness which fills so much of our daily routine. There is little to delight the senses when we operate a computer keyboard or drive a car through crowded city streets. Our children learn how to enhance their cognitive skills, but not how to awaken their aesthetic sense. All of us live lives that are starved of beauty, and one of the prime functions of a Soul Garden is to overcome this dearth by regaling our senses with the sights, sounds and smells of nature.

Philosophers may argue about the exact nature of the aesthetic experience, but all agree that the appreciation of beauty is accompanied by feelings of contentment and delight. 'A thing of beauty is a joy for ever,' wrote Keats. We experience this rapture when we watch a magnificent sunset, inhale the heady perfume of a lilac bush or study the intricate patterning of a butterfly's wing. A Soul Garden should be designed to maximize these sensuous delights.

CHAPTER SEVEN

The Pleasure Garden

'God Almighty first planted a garden; and, indeed, it is the purest of human pleasures.'

FRANCIS BACON, 'OF GARDENS'

A LITTLE OF WHAT YOU FANCY DOES YOU GOOD, OR SO SAID doctors in the past. Now we're encouraged to believe that everything pleasurable – eating, drinking and idle relaxation – carries a health risk. To keep fit today we must be prepared to suffer. We must exercise until we feel the burn, and keep slim by eating calorie-reduced foods which taste like shredded cardboard. Yet there is ample medical evidence to prove that health and happiness go hand in hand. Professor David Warburton, head of the department of human psycho-pharmacology at Reading University, has made a special study of the physiological effects of mood changes. He concludes: 'Happy people live longer and are healthier.' This fact ought to influence our approach to gardening, which should always be a fun activity. However tough the tasks we tackle, they should be treated as playful pastimes rather than onerous chores.

We have only one life to live and it is up to us to enjoy that one short spell. Every minute we spend feeling miserable is sixty seconds when we could have been having a thoroughly good time. We should forget the killjoy preaching of the Puritans and turn instead to the teaching of the Lord Buddha, who said that man's highest goal was to secure the happiness of all living beings. Many of the early philosophers argued that the major purpose of the arts is to add to the total sum of human pleasure. If this is true of music, poetry and painting, why should it not be equally true of garden-ing, which is in many ways more likely to provide a wide range of sensual delights? Happiness is not a sin, it is a worthy aim, and one of the prime functions of a Soul Garden is to serve as a source of pleasure and play.

In Britain, two out of every three people have a garden. It is often a treasured amenity, for many people take delight in making things grow and love to potter in the open air and watch the changing seasons. But for others the garden is an unwelcome burden. A 1993 poll of *Daily Telegraph* readers revealed that over a quarter of British gardeners found gardening a chore from which they got little or no enjoyment. They kept their gardens tidy but only out of duty. Such people are unlikely to read this book, which is a pity because their lives would be so much richer and happier if they developed their gardens as places to play in and enjoy themselves.

Epicurus, who founded the Epicurean school of philosophy in the third century BC, spent a large part of his time in his garden, some distance from his town house in Athens. While walking in this peaceful haven he developed his ideas on nature, virtue, holiness and the good life, and it was within the walls of this garden that he taught his disciples, who became known as the Garden Philosophers. Far from being a debauched libertine, Epicurus ate sparingly and found no time for sexual promiscuity. Nevertheless he had no doubt that man's primary duty was to be happy: 'Pleasure', he said, 'is the beginning and end of the blessed life.' It was this contentment that he sought throughout his life, and which he cultivated with such success that on his deathbed, even though he was racked with pain, he could still talk of 'the joy in my heart'. That joy and contentment can be found within a Soul Garden.

A PLACE TO PLAY

GARDENS, IF THEY ARE TO FULFIL THEIR THERAPEUTIC FUNCTION, must be places of fun. For some people gardening is largely a cerebral activity, a serious matter of testing the acidity of the soil and fixing Latin name tags to rare plants. But there is little doubt that Saint Dorothy, the patron saint of gardeners, bestows her finest fruits on those who garden with their hearts as well as their heads. Some of the world's most famous gardens incorporated whimsical elements which were designed to evoke a smile or an outright belly laugh. When Peter the Great created his marvellous gardens at Peterhof, in St Petersburg, he included a fake 'oak tree' which sprays water on unsuspecting passers-by. This appealed to his rumbustious sense of humour, and still affords amusement for the thousands of people who visit the gardens every year. The drawing books of William Kent contain numerous jokes in a similar vein. Here and there, amid the grand fountains, temples and obelisks, he would place a statue of dancing rabbits, urinating dogs or chickens banding together to hang a fox from a tree. All these artefacts were introduced to make his clients laugh.

At a sheltered spot in my garden I have built a 'gnome home', a diminutive temple with truncated columns and a Doric architrave which is just large enough to offer shelter to a gnome who has been in the family for many years. The discovery of this unexpected feature never fails to provoke a smile from visitors, unless they are botanical purists who are shocked by this lapse of horticultural decorum. But why do we so despise garden gnomes? (They have been banned from the Chelsea Flower Show for reasons which a spokesman for the Royal Horticultural Society admits are purely snobbish.) These sprightly creatures are figures of fun, innocent reminders of the elves and pixies which were once thought to inhabit every garden nook and woodland cranny. If gnomes cause mirth they should be encouraged, for laughter and play are two of the most potent therapies known to man.

Play was central to Plato's philosophy of life. He once asked his students the rhetorical question, 'What then is the right way of living?' – to which he gave the immediate response, 'Life must be lived as play.' We suffer today because of the deadly earnestness of our lives. We have little time for fun and even less time for play, unless it takes the form of an organized sport, played to strict rules and in a keen competitive spirit. We too seldom let our hair down and give vent to our animal spirits. Yet this release is vital to our emotional well-being, as psychiatrist Erik Erikson discovered in 1964 when he carried out a prolonged personality study of a group of youngsters. He first examined his subjects when they were at school, and then thirty years later he tested them again when they had grown up and were well established in their adult careers. One of the most surprising findings of this investigation was that the subjects who were leading the most interesting, fulfilling lives were the ones who had managed to retain a sense of playfulness.

This playfulness is more easily displayed outdoors than in the more formal settings of offices, shops, libraries and churches. Every time we enter a garden we should try to do so in a child-like frame of mind, with a sense of wonder and excitement. Tests reveal that when adults are asked to describe a garden, they invariably concentrate on its physical layout. They picture it in terms of its size, shape and architectural features, plants, lawns, hedges and paths. But when children describe a garden, they think of it primarily as a playground. They are not interested in the things the garden *has*, so much as the things it lets them *do*: whether they can hunt for worms, play hide-and-seek, have football matches on the lawn, climb trees and use the see-saw they have made from discarded planks of wood. A Soul Garden should be planned with this in mind, not merely as an aesthetically pleasing structure but as a place where we can have fun.

When Henry VIII built the palace of Nonsuch in Surrey, he gave orders that its grounds should be filled with numerous diversions including tennis courts, archery butts and a bowling green. If we are to escape the stress of everyday life, our gardens should provide similar inducement for fun and games. However small our plots may be, we can probably still find space for a swing or basketball hoop. If we have more room, we may opt for a putting green, a boules court or a croquet lawn.

The sixteenth-century French satirist François Rabelais, author of *Gargantua* and *Pantagruel*, gives a clear idea of his concept of an ideal world. He describes the Abbey of Thélème as a temple devoted to pleasure. Above the Great Gate is an inscription banning entry to all killjoys, hypocrites, bigots, snivellers, office holders, scribes, pharisees and misers. In the abbey's pleasure gardens there is a wide variety of lively enter-tainments – a theatre, a swimming pool, tennis courts, archery butts, a falconry and riding stables. All is given over to the pursuit of happiness, for the abbey has one overriding principle: 'Do what you wish is the whole of the law.' On the face of it, this sounds an outrageously libertine precept, and yet it contains more than a scintilla of sound advice. For much of the time we are serving the needs of others, unable to relax or to 'do our own thing'. In a garden we can afford the luxury of pleasing ourselves, in a way which causes no offence to others. When Peter the Great came to London, travelling incognito under the name Pyotr Mikhailov, he took a house called Sayes Court on the south bank of the Thames. By day he was working under considerable pressure, secretly studying the ships being built at the Royal Docks in nearby Deptford, but at night when he returned to the safety of the gardens of Sayes Court he relaxed by holding wheelbarrow races with his friends. Whenever tension mounts, we need the release that uninhibited outdoor play can bring.

Life is a terminal condition. None of us knows for sure how long we will live, so why should we wait until we are facing death before we find time to take our pleasures? A journey of self-discovery can begin in a garden as readily as on a psychiatrist's couch. Here we can let go of worldly cares and achieve completeness, finding both happiness and personal identity. The Chinese, who recognize how closely linked these two concepts are, use the same word, *tsetch*, to mean 'to be happy' and 'to have found oneself'.

THE WOODFIELD EXPERIMENT

THE IDEAL GARDEN SHOULD APPEAL DIRECTLY TO THE SENSES. IT should be totally and unashamedly sybaritic. Even though we bombard our sense organs with synthetic perfumes, flashing lights, flavour-enhanced foods and wall-to-wall canned music, we are starved of true sensory pleasure. We are over-stimulated, and yet we suffer from sensory deprivation because we have exchanged quantity for quality. Science encourages us to take a wholly rational view of the world, to approach it with our intellect rather than to experience it first hand through our five senses. We expect to learn the truth from books and films rather than by a process of personal discovery. As a result our sensory perceptions are failing and we are losing faith in our own powers of observation. We admire the skill of native trackers and often credit them with a 'sixth sense', whereas their proficiency in fact stems from making full use of the faculties we all possess, of sight, hearing, taste, smell and touch.

Our lives would be infinitely richer if we developed the acuity of these senses. The Human Potential movement, which flourished in the 1970s, encouraged people to become more sensual in order to achieve a heightened state of consciousness. Consciousness-raising courses urged people to 'Go for a hike in the woods . . . Cook a meal out of doors . . . enjoy the aroma of the smoke and the special taste of the charcoal-grilled food . . . Listen to the rustle of the leaves . . . feel the touch of the wind on your face.' While these courses were of great value for many people, experienced gardeners have little need of training in sensual development for these are sensations they experience every day of their lives.

One of the simplest and most effective ways of increasing sensory awareness is through the form of relaxation therapy known as 'guided imagery'. Patients are helped to escape their tensions by making a fantasy journey to a private Shangri-La where all is harmony and peace. They may be invited to imagine that they are lying in a flower-filled country meadow, where they can run their fingers through the grass, smell the fragrance of the flowers and hear the singing of the birds and the gentle murmur of a nearby stream. This focus on pleasurable sensations is the perfect antidote for stress, a salve which can be applied every time we contemplate an individual flower or a garden or a pleasing natural landscape. When Pliny, the great Roman historian, retired to his Laurentine Villa, he rested his mind by soaking up the magnificent views over flower-filled meadows, across the bay of Ostia to the mountains towering in the distance. If we use our imaginations, we can benefit from this form of relaxation before we reach the age of retirement.

To heighten their potential for pleasure, gardens should be structured in such a way that they offer the maximum possible sensory stimulation. Oscar Wilde, well known for his light and witty epigrams, also made observations of great profundity. As one of the world's most cultivated aesthetes, he observed: 'Nothing can cure the soul but the senses, just as nothing can cure the senses but the soul.' We need to make better use of our sensory faculties, otherwise we run the risk of making a complete 'non-sense' of our lives.

Field trials have shown that the sensory stimulation provided by gardening can exert a highly therapeutic effect. Most of the children at the Woodfield Nursery School in Oldham had severe health problems and learning difficulties, and many had spent a lot of time indoors, either confined to a hospital ward or lying in bed at home. In 1995 workers at the school raised sufficient money to turn the tarmac playground into a sensory garden. 'The basic idea was to create areas of sound, touch, colour, taste and smell through the use of natural material like herbs, plants, stones and wood,' one of the organizers explained. The intention was to make the garden a place where the children and their families could relax and enjoy the gentle stimulus of the natural sights and scents. The blossoming of the tarmac had a striking effect. Infants who had previously been withdrawn and resistant to mental stimulation could now be contacted through their bodily senses. One severely handicapped boy reacted with chuckles and broad grins every time he felt the breeze blowing on his face. 'To be able to take him round the garden on a gentle windy day gave him and his carers great pleasure,' reported one of the school's nurses in an article published in the *Nursing Times*. Such has been the success of this venture that observers from all over Britain are now attending workshops devoted to the Woodfield approach to sensory stimulation.

We all have much to gain from heightening our powers of sensual perception. The sensual person is invariably en- thusiastic, while the non-sensual person tends to be apathetic – a word derived from the Greek *a-pathos*, meaning 'without feeling'. The sensual person looks out on a world of beauty, whereas the non-sensual person views life in drab monotones. To rediscover the beauty of the world we need to embrace it with the warmth and passion of our senses, rather than with the remote, robotic arms of conscious thought.

THE MUSIC OF THE SPHERES

GARDENS MUST BE PLEASING TO THE EYE, AS THE LAST CHAPTER emphasized, but they must also be gratifying to the senses of sound and smell. One of the most exhaustive textbooks of garden design ever published was Christian Hirschfeld's five- volume *Théorie de l'art des jardins*, which appeared in 1779. Here it was stated that 'a grove embellished by fresh foliage and smiling prospects is even more delightful when at the same time we hear the song of the nightingale, the murmur of a waterfall, and when we breathe the sweet odour of violets.' This triple appeal is the basis of sensory garden design.

Ever since the invention of the printing press, and even more so since the advent of electronic data storage and retrieval, the eye rather than the ear has been our main source of information. The opposite was true of earlier, pastoral societies, when people's existence depended primarily on the acuteness of their hearing. Neanderthal man, who lived in forests and overgrown savannahs, *heard* the approach of dangerous predators long before they hove into view. Studies carried out by Professor R. Murray Schafer, Professor of Communication Studies at Simon Fraser University, British Columbia, suggest that the 'soundscapes' of primitive cultures contained 69 per cent natural sounds, 26 per cent sounds made by the human voice, and 5 per cent noise of primitive tools. The balance of noise we hear today is totally different. In 1973, when Schafer completed his work, natural sounds comprised only 6 per cent of the overall volume of background noise. The rest was made up of 26 per cent human sounds and 68 per cent the noise of cars, sirens, aircraft, broadcasting media and machinery. Today the balance has shifted further still, leaving us with a deafening preponderance of technological noise.

We have spent millions of pounds creating near-perfect systems of music reproduction. The cardinal feature of a CD player is that it has a very favourable signal-to-background-noise ratio, which means that the musical notes we wish to hear are not obliterated by the scrapes, hisses, bumps and booms which we used to get in the early days of wind-up gramophones. But we cannot say the same for the sound quality of our everyday lives, where we have created and, worse still, come to tolerate a distressingly poor acoustic environment. In a modern town we can no longer hear the signal – human speech, bird-song or the rustle of the wind in the trees – for the deafening background noise.

Vienna was a bustling commercial centre in Mozart's day and yet it still retained its medieval peace. Fire warnings could be transmitted even to people living on the outskirts of the town by the shout of a warden, posted at the top of St Steven's Cathedral. Now we use klaxons for fire alarms and the horns need to be made more powerful as the level of background noise mounts. When they were first introduced, the sirens of police cars and fire engines were designed to emit a sound level of 88 decibels at fifty feet. Now they are made to produce an ear-shattering 122 decibels at a distance of only ten feet. We are provided with eyelids to act as shields against unwanted light, but haven't yet developed ear flaps to shut out unwanted sounds.

The musical education of *Homo sapiens* began the moment we started to listen to natural sounds. According to Greek mythology, the lyre was invented when Hermes heard the sound of the wind resonating through a turtle shell, and Pan, the god of nature, was known for his love of melody. He carried a syrinx, the legendary pipes of Pan, made from seven reeds through which the wind blew to make the seven sounds of heavenly music. Pythagoras, however, claimed that the origin of the music of the spheres lay in the planetary bodies, which emitted a humming sound as they revolved. Religious mystics dance to yet another tune. They believe that every living creature emits a song, which persists as an echo when they die. The distant sounds we hear when we communicate with nature are, they say, these sound traces reverberating through the great void of time and space. To the Celts, the heavenly music is made by the unseen fairy folk. For them the *genius loci*, or spirit of a garden, is expressed in the sound the nymphs and dryads make as they stir the wind, rustle the leaves and ripple the water.

One great virtue of a garden is that it takes us away from the clangour of today's cities and gives us a chance once more to listen to the song of a thrush, the humming of bees, the rustle of aspen leaves and the trickle of water cascading from a fountain. In a Soul Garden we should foster natural sounds by planting grasses and trees which whisper in the wind, creating waterfalls and fountains, and erecting Japanese wind chimes and aeolian harps which respond to the lightest breeze. The Chinese used to breed crickets because they enjoyed the music they made. The very least that we can do is to put out nesting boxes and food to attract regular visits from songbirds.

Above all we need time to enjoy the delights of nature, time not only to smell the roses but also to listen to these heavenly sounds. When Sir Walter Raleigh sailed up the Orinoco river in 1595 he heard the sweet singing of the indigenous birds and thought that he had entered paradise. If we want to create a paradise here on earth, we must occasionally blot out the deafening roar of internal combustion engines, police sirens, vacuum cleaners, phones and ghetto blasters and listen once more to the music of the spheres.

HEAVEN SCENT

ONE OF THE GREATEST JOYS OF GARDENING IS THAT IT ENCOURAGES us to quicken our sense of smell. This faculty is little used today

– except by industrial psychologists, who have discovered the potential of perfumes to motivate staff and sell goods. Some firms have started to release scents into the air-conditioning system of offices, so that employees are invigorated by stimulating odours in the morning and relaxed by sedative oils towards the end of the working day. Seductive odours are also being employed as subliminal marketing tools. Trials show that perfumed packs of ladies' tights sell more quickly than identical packs which do not carry the alluring scent. Perfume is powerful stuff, and equally potent medicine, especially in the hands of knowledgeable aromatherapists.

At one time it was fashionable to overload gardens with scent, a vogue which reached absurdity in eighteenth-century France. One of the great advocates of 'odoriferous sensuality' was René-Louis Girardin, who in 1777 wrote a book called *De la composition des paysages*, which encouraged people to fill their gardens with the scent of tuberose, jonquil and violets. The gardeners appointed to stock the grounds of the Grand Trianon, the country retreat of King Louis XIV, were a trifle too exuberant in following Girardin's advice. They packed the parterres with 125,000 flowerpots filled with scented flowers. The effect was so overpowering, and the tuberose so pungent, that the King and his courtiers were forced to take to boats to escape the overwhelming smell around the house.

A Soul Garden needs to be subtle in its use of perfume, although it cannot afford to be too restrained because of the weakness of our olfactory sense. A bee can smell an apple tree at a distance of two miles; we would be lucky to pick up its scent even if it was only a few feet from our nose! Our problems with scent started when we developed an upright posture. This raised the human nose several feet above the ground, which makes it more useful as a perch for spectacles than an olfactory organ. At this level it is too high to smell the roses, too distant to track the spores of animals and too remote even to pick up the genital scents of potential mates.

If we want to enjoy the smell of the flowers in our gardens – lavender, stocks, roses, violets and herbs – we must be prepared to get down on our haunches and sniff. This we should do routinely every time we wander round a garden. It's a splendid exercise for the soul, and equally good for the hips and knees. Once you're down at ground level close to the flowers, breathe in really deeply so that the odour traces are drawn up to the top of your nose where the olfactory cells are housed. Do this several times before you move on to sample the next fragrant leaf or flower. This is also a useful technique for smokers who are anxious to kick the nicotine habit. Dr Donald Frederickson, director of the New York Smoking Withdrawal Clinics, gets his clients to mimic the action of smoking whenever they feel the craving to smoke, and finds that by breathing deeply through the nose and then slowly exhaling, they get almost the same satisfaction and relaxation as they obtain from drawing on a cigarette.

Sampling the scents of a garden is a joy which shouldn't be hurried. It is an exercise which will often trigger off a chain of long-lost memories. Just as the smell of madeleine cakes helped Marcel Proust to recapture the memories of times past, so the scent of newly mown grass or an autumn bonfire can help us recall our own private history.

When we revisit these memories at leisure, and slowly explore the sensory pleasures of nature, we experience a very special sense of spiritual harmony and peace. In *Walden*, Henry David Thoreau gives his account of the period in the 1840s when he lived alone in a cabin in an isolated wood on the outskirts of Concord, Massachusetts. He relates how one night while he was wandering around Walden Pond in his shirtsleeves he felt an overwhelming sense of cosmic unity. As he watched the wind rippling on the water, heard the bullfrogs calling and listened to the rustling of the alder and poplar trees, he experienced that delicious oceanic feeling 'when the whole body is one sense, and imbibes delight through every pore'. Those precious moments cannot be produced on demand, but may arise unforced within a Soul Garden.

A PLACE OF NOSTALGIA, ROMANCE AND WONDER

TO WORK ITS FULL MAGIC THE GARDEN WE ARE DEVISING NEEDS TO be not only sensuous but also highly romantic. It must be structured to stimulate the senses *and* the imagination. Essentially a work of fantasy, a place where we can dream, gaze at the stars and eat honey and wild strawberries, it is far removed from the laboratories of the horticultural boffins. Here plants are not fed on chemical nutrients but grow by magic, like Jack's beanstalk. This is a wild, natural haven populated by elves and fairies rather than by aphids, sawflies, gall mites and thrips. Here flowers are called by their folk names – key of heaven, Jack-in-the-pulpit and love-lies-bleeding – rather than classified by their staid Latin names of *Primula veris*, *Arum triphyllum* and *Viola tricolor*. Our urgent need today is for gardens which offer a total escape from the rigour and discipline of the assembly line and the electronic office; gardens which celebrate the bounty of nature rather than the brilliance of technological science. This natural wonderland can be created with even the most modest purse, and in the tiniest space, for wonder is a product of the subjective outlook rather than the objective view. As Rachel Carson wrote in *The Sense of Wonder*, 'Wherever you are and whatever your resources, you can still look up at the sky – its dawn and twilight beauties, its moving clouds, its stars by night. You can listen to the wind, whether it blows with majestic voice through a forest or sings a many-voiced chorus around the eaves of your house or apartment building.'

The observation of these natural beauties will bring romance and harmony into our lives even if we live in the most derelict city precinct. When we catch sight of the sun rising above a pall of early morning mist we are transported at once into another realm, a world of simplicity and innocence. Often our thoughts go back to a time when we first saw such sights. As a young boy in the 1780s William Hazlitt, the essayist, was frequently taken by his father on trips to the Montpelier Tea Gardens at Walworth. Years later he could still picture the gardens: the beds of larkspur, the tall holly oaks, the bees buzzing around the sunflowers, the box-tree borders, the gravel walks and painted alcove. 'All that I have observed since, of flowers and plants, and grass-plots, and of suburb delights, seem to me, borrowed from "that first garden of my innocence",' he wrote. These are priceless memories which never fade.

This nostalgic appeal can be strengthened by stocking the garden with reminders of bygone days: a shrub brought back from a favourite holiday, the gravestone of a beloved pet, a cutting from the Virginia creeper that grew around your grand-parents' house, the swing you played on as a child, the bench where your parents sat on the patio of your family home. The sight of these objects should provoke a smile of quiet content-ment and trigger off a chain of happy recollections. My present garden is festooned with wild strawberries, which tumble over stone walls, grow from cracks in paved pathways and act as rampant ground-cover plants in shrub borders. They are there to serve as a romantic aide-mémoire, for the wild strawberry has always been regarded as a symbol of seduction and sensu-ality, which is why it so often features in the voluptuous paintings of Sandro Botticelli. But those sweet, sensual berries have a more personal significance for me. Some months before we were married, my wife and I took a trip to Venice. Everything about that holiday was memorable, but especially the sunny day we spent on the tiny island of Torcello, where we lunched in the gardens of the famous Cipriani restaurant. I remember little about the meal, except that it ended with a delicious bowl of wild strawberries, the first I had ever tasted. Now, when I saunter around my garden and sample those exquisite berries, my mind goes back to that idyllic holiday and I feel a warm nostalgic glow.

Others stock their gardens with inanimate mementoes. Clementine Churchill took a four-month cruise to Indonesia, leaving her famous husband at home to finish writing a book, and while she was away she had a brief but tender holiday romance. When the trip was over, her lover presented her with a pink Bali dove in a wicker cage as a souvenir of their time together. When the dove died she buried it under the sundial in the walled gardens of Chartwell, with an inscription which reads:

It does not do to wander
Too far from sober men,
But there's an island yonder,
I think of it again.

In later life, whenever she walked the grounds of Chartwell and saw those words, they brought back sentimental recollections of that pretty Bali dove, her debonair lover Terence Philip and the enchanting cruise they shared through the East Indian islands.

CAUSE FOR CELEBRATION

SENSUOUS GARDENS WHICH ARE CREATED AS PLACES OF ROMANCE and beauty should perhaps carry a government health warning, for if they are full of pleasing sights, sounds and alluring scents they can exert a powerful aphrodisiac effect. It is no coincidence that Venus, the goddess of beauty and romance, was at one time also worshipped as the goddess of gardens. History shows that most places of pleasure, from public baths to communal parks, have also been centres of erotic arousal.

During the Middle Ages sex was often celebrated out of doors, partly because it seemed more romantic and exciting, but more especially because the open air afforded a modicum of privacy in an age when homes were cramped and beds were commonly placed in the living room and shared with several members of the family. Many of the illustrations on the early astrological calendars show people making love in the fresh air, particularly at the onset of spring. At this time it was customary for couples to go into the fields to mate; according to the principles of sympathetic magic, if they did this they would ensure the fertility of the land. The May Day celebrations served the same function. On this day young girls and boys met and went into the woods to welcome the dawn. The ostensible reason for their trip was to collect handfuls of spring greenery to decorate the village, but for many it was a heaven-sent opportunity to indulge themselves in an act which in turn would assure the fecundity of the earth.

It was not only in the spring that the more intimate courtship behaviour had to take place in fields or in the secluded arbours of town gardens. A contemporary record gives an unequivocal account of these amorous goings-on: 'In the Feeldes and Suburbes their Gardens are locked, some of them have three or fower keys a piece . . . one they keep for themselves, the other their Paramours have to go in before them . . . where they, meeting their sweet hartes, receive their wished desires.'

With the arrival of the Romantic movement, there was an added incentive to use the garden as a place of erotic adventure. The great gardens of the eighteenth century drew their inspiration from the landscape paintings of Botticelli, Poussin and Claude Lorraine, which were peopled by voluptuous naked figures reclining in languid poses, sipping wine, eating grapes and listening to the celestial music of harp and flute. In the background were the mythical symbols of profane love – Pan, Eros, Bacchus, cupids, satyrs and nymphs. It is not surprising that the people who sought to recreate these pastoral scenes were also inspired to recapture the same bucolic pleasures.

Picnic sex – love among scented, flower-strewn fields – has been a romantic dream of city dwellers for generations but in the eighteenth century it became a practical possibility. Scented flowers were introduced into town gardens to facilitate the act of seduction, in the belief that sensual arousal was an inexorable first step to sexual arousal. Some observers noted that the facial expression women adopt when they smell a flower is practically identical to the one they show at the height of erotic stimulation, and one expert maintained that the inhalation of powerful flowers scents could provoke an orgasm. Secluded buildings were introduced into gardens to provide trysting spots for lovers. Sir William Davenant's romantic painting 'The Shepherd's Paradise' shows a wooded mount, bearing a pagoda-like building which is clearly marked the 'Lover's Cabinet'. Sir Francis Dashwood went one step further and developed an erotic garden at West Wycombe with a temple of Venus and a sensuous cave with a vagina-shaped entrance. Other land-owners were less tolerant of these horticultural high jinks. One of the unusual features of William Shenstone's garden in Yorkshire was a delightful root house. Here guests were invited to rest but not to dally. In fact the arbour carried an inscription which read: 'Harm betide the wayward swain, who dares our hallow'd haunts profane.'

The majority of adults today have probably never made love out of doors, unless it is in a lay-by on the back seat of a car. But deep down there remains a feeling that there is something special about love in the open air. Romantic novelists have no doubt that alfresco sex is more spontaneous, free and un-inhibited. In Thomas Hardy's *Tess of the D'Urbervilles* the young heroine gives her all amid 'rabbits hopping', and in *Lady Chatterley's Lover* Mellors makes a flower arrangement between Connie's naked thighs as a prelude to their union. Such raptures were naturally anathema to the Puritans, who regarded gardens as sinful places because of the temptations they evoked. St Anselm, Archbishop of Canterbury, had taken a similar stand many centuries before, when he warned his followers that gardens were dangerous because of the pleasures they aroused and the senses they stimulated. But there seems little harm in sensual arousal in a garden, providing it is between consenting adults, and doesn't alarm the neighbours, damage the daisies or frighten the horses.

In a sensual garden we find happiness because we take delight in everyday things. By focusing on the simple pleasures of the here and now – the gaiety, fun and sensory delights – we forget the complications of yesterday and the conjectured problems of tomorrow. When we wander into a Soul Garden and give full rein to our senses we find contentment, and provide confirmation of the soundness of the old adage: 'If you want to be happy for a night get drunk, for a year get married, and for a lifetime get a garden.'

rest & r

The health of workaholics suffers not because they are oppressed by a surfeit of work, but because they have a deficit of fun and games. Wise people make a good life as well as a good living, aiming to enjoy the pleasures of the here and now rather than constantly to follow a policy of deferred gratification. So they find time to smell the roses, to have fun cooking barbecue meals or simply to be in a hammock gazing idly at the clouds.

A prime function of a Soul Garden is to satisfy our need for periods of rest and relax-ation. So many gardens are allowed to become places of unrelieved toil, where there are always more jobs to be done than there is time to complete them. A Soul Garden, on the other hand, should be designed to serve as a pleasure ground, a sybaritic hide-away where we can relax, let our hair down, play games, hold parties or simply revel in the enjoyment of a wide array of natural scents and sounds.

CHAPTER EIGHT

A Breath of
Fresh Air

'Happy the man whose wish and care
A few paternal acres bound,
Content to breathe his native air,
In his own ground.'

ALEXANDER POPE, 'ODE ON SOLITUDE'

*C*OUNTLESS BOOKS HAVE BEEN WRITTEN DESCRIBING THE social consequences of the great human migration which took place at the time of the Industrial Revolution, when masses of peasants left the countryside to find work in the newly developing towns. But few writers and historians have considered one aspect of this translocation which has had a marked effect on our physical well-being. Two centuries ago the vast majority of the population worked out of doors. Nowadays most people spend the bulk of their time indoors, in rooms which are starved of natural sunlight and where the air is often stagnant, dry and overheated. These living conditions can play havoc with our health.

In the Middle Ages nobody was short of fresh air, for whether one lived in town or country there was little opportunity, or incentive, to stay indoors. Most medieval families lived and slept in one sparsely furnished room. Artificial light was poor and costly, which meant that work was generally performed outside. Chimney stacks didn't appear until the sixteenth century so even the homes of the landed gentry had holes in the roof to permit the escape of smoke from open hearths. On fine days people found it more agreeable to take their leisure out of doors, where they could bask in the warmth of the sun's rays, which provide as much heat as a one-bar electric fire for every square yard of earth.

Nowadays it is customary to regard the garden as an extension of the house but our forebears had the reverse perspective. They lived, worked and played in the open air and retreated to their homes – tree houses, caves, igloos, tepees or mud huts – only when they were in need of shelter. They hunted, foraged, herded and tilled out of doors. And when their working day was over it was under the open skies that they feasted, danced, held their ceremonial powwows and performed their religious rites. We have exchanged their freedom and exhilarating pastoral lifestyle for the comforts of our centrally heated, draught-excluding, double-glazed cocoons.

Surveys show that most people in Western countries today spend 85–90 per cent of their time indoors. We have barely begun to assess the impact of this major change. At present our attention is so firmly fixed on the problems caused by the pollution of the outside environment that we tend to ignore the insidious hazards resulting from pollution of the indoor air. We pay scant attention to the revelations about Sick Building Syndrome, and disregard the medical reports which show that children living in centrally heated homes have 50 per cent more hay fever and asthma than those living in homes warmed by open fires. Our living conditions have undergone a dramatic change. We have become a new species – *Homo encapsularis* – and are beginning to suffer the consequences of this mollycoddled, hothouse living. Yet we can lessen the effects of this hermetically sealed lifestyle by making a conscious effort to spend more time out of doors.

As a tonic it may be undervalued today, but in Victorian times the health-conscious middle classes went to inordinate lengths to bathe their bodies and fill their lungs with invigorating fresh air. In those days it was considered vital to sleep in bedrooms where the windows were flung wide open to the elements. 'The body will not be hardened, or empowered to resist the attacks of disease, unless there be thorough ventilation of the bedroom,' wrote Dr Gustave Jaeger, the German professor of physiology who became better known as the manufacturer of Jaeger clothing. Another health guru, Dr Harvey Kellogg, supported this view and designed a range of bedroom balconies and fresh air dormitories in America so that debilitated patients could rebuild their health with regular doses of good night air. He argued that men and women were by nature outdoor dwellers, and suffered a wide range of ailments when they moved indoors and were deprived of the energizing stimulus of sunshine and fresh air.

This craze for fresh air therapy was a natural reaction, for the Victorians were the first to suffer the full impact of stifling city living, and so were easily persuaded of the need to eat, sleep and work out of doors. In fact, doctors in nineteenth-century Britain, one of the first countries to suffer the debilitating side effects of the Industrial Revolution, seized every opportunity to promote the virtues of aerial baths and aerotherapy. Arcades were built so that shoppers could stroll in the open air, whatever the weather, and feast their eyes on the growing range of novelties in the stores. Architects designed houses according to the new aerist theories, building porticoes for shelter so that their wealthier clients could enjoy their gardens on rainy days. The poor were urged to keep their windows open day and night, even if they were living in the heavily polluted air of an industrial city. One Scottish doctor, an avid sanitary reformer, made a regular practice of breaking the window panes of his poorer patients' homes, so that they were scoured by cleansing blasts of outside air.

To maximize our health, we need to be in an environment where the air flows freely. The Western poets and philosophers of the nineteenth century were enthusiastic supporters of the outdoor movement. Multitudes were inspired by the nature poems of William Wordsworth, which described his wanderings over the windswept dales of Cumberland, where his spirits were lifted by the sight of fluttering daffodils, dappled turf, venerable trees, mossy stones and small, sweet celandines. On the other side of the Atlantic, Henry David Thoreau wrote of his passion for the woodsman's life, which invigorated his body and provided a ready cure for his bouts of melancholia. 'We must go out and re-ally ourselves to Nature every day,' he urged. 'I am sensible that I am imbibing health when I open my mouth to the wind. Staying in the house breeds a sort of insanity.'

John Ruskin, the leader of the Victorian Aesthetic Movement, insisted that the prime duty of politicians was not to build prestigious opera houses, museums and art galleries, but to provide town dwellers with fresh air and congenial places where they could walk. This message eventually got through to the nation's town planners, who came to regard parks and gardens as hygienic necessities for the masses rather than superfluous luxuries for the favoured few.

Several enlightened industrialists joined this crusade, providing their employees with garden villages, such as Lever's Port Sunlight and Cadbury's Bourneville, built on open land well beyond the factory gates. Even politicians were stirred to take action. In Britain a 'fresh air tax' was instituted to raise funds to establish green belts and public pleasure gardens, which were soon dubbed the 'lungs' of the city. A similar initiative in Germany, known as the Schrebergärten movement, provided people living in crowded tenement blocks with patches of vacant land outside the town for use as allotments.

By this time fresh air therapy had gained the full support of the medical establishment, and had the backing of such eminent men as Sir Leonard Hill, adviser to Britain's Medical Research Council. In his massive report, *The Science of Ventilation and Open Air Treatment* (1920), Hill wrote: 'The ideal conditions out of doors are seen to promote the feeling of comfort and happiness, a gentle cooling breeze to promote adequate cooling of the skin and stimulate the metabolism of the body.' In more recent times Dr Gordon Latto, one of the pioneers of holistic medicine in Britain, also embraced the regular use of air baths and outdoor exercise. One of his most famous patients was Sir Francis Chichester, who sought Nature Cure treatment for his lung cancer. Latto prescribed a wholesome blend of vegetarian food, herbal remedies and fresh air. Chichester adopted this regime with unbounded enthusiasm and decided, at the age of sixty-five, to embark on a single-handed circumnavigation of the globe in his tiny yacht *Gipsy Moth* to make sure that his lungs and body got the maximum possible exposure to fresh air. When the trip was over, tests were carried out which showed that the tumour had gone into spontaneous remission. Another of Gordon Latto's eminent patients was the historian Sir George Trevelyan, an elderly man whose arthritis was severely limiting his ability to walk. On Latto's advice Sir George had a large grass mound created in his garden, which he made a practice of climbing every day. This regular outdoor exercise strengthened his legs to such an extent that within a short while he was able to join Latto on a successful climbing expedition to the summit of Mount Snowdon.

WHOLESOME CURRENTS

STALE AIR HAS LONG BEEN SEEN AS A HAZARD. THE PHYSICIANS OF the eighteenth century undoubtedly had some strange ideas about it, believing it to be filled with harmful miasmas and noxious 'animal steams'. But they also made some very sound observations about the need for fresh air ventilation. For instance, a treatise published in 1733, *The Effects of Air on Human Bodies*, recommended that 'Private houses ought to be perflated once a Day, by opening Doors and Windows, to blow off the Animal Steams.' The same book warned that houses which are kept warm and are 'fenc'd from Wind, and where the Carpenter's Work is so nice as to exclude all outward Air, are not the most wholesom'. This advice stands true today, for there is little doubt that many modern buildings are too well insulated for our good.

Static air in draught-proof homes and offices often seems enervating and stale. This feeling is often attributed to a lack of oxygen caused by the constant breathing of recycled air. In Victorian times people were urged to keep windows open in bedrooms and offices to replenish the oxygen supply. 'There is not a bedroom in the land which contains sufficient air to last one sleeper the whole night,' argued one sanitary reformer. The problem was thought to be even worse in public banqueting halls and ballrooms, where human lungs were forced to compete with hundreds of burning candles for a limited supply of oxygen. No doubt the air in these places did feel devitalized and musty, but this was never due to oxygen depletion. Tests show that it is possible to reduce the oxygen content of a room until a match cannot be lit, without the occupants feeling in any way uncomfortable. In fact the oxygen content of the air rarely falls by more than 1 per cent in a crowded room, whereas it would need to fall by a full 4 per cent before it became too low to support the burning of matches and candles, and a further 3 per cent before it produced symptoms of stuffiness and exhaustion. We may feel listless in enclosed environments but this is only because of the stillness of the air. Set a fan operating and the lethargy quickly disappears.

In the 1920s and 1930s doctors were still prescribing holidays according to the biological needs of their patients. Patients who were exhausted were sent to relaxing resorts, often set in hollows, where there was little circulation of air. Those who were enervated were directed to invigorating coastal resorts where they would be stimulated by the buffeting of the wind. Seaside towns which were fully exposed to the blast of the north-east wind, such as Scarborough and Skegness, were promoted for their 'bracing' properties. Nowadays our views have changed. The currents of air which our grandparents welcomed as health-giving have been reclassified as noxious draughts, which we shun in the mistaken belief that they are harbingers of all manner of diseases, from the common cold to more serious rheumatic ailments. We choose to live and work in an enervating fug, which saps our vitality and reduces our alertness. Airline companies manipulate the energy levels of their passengers by controlling the flow of cabin air. On long-haul flights, when they want them to sleep to give the cabin staff a rest, they simply cut down the rate of air circulation. This simple but effective form of control demonstrates how accustomed we are to living with poor ventilation.

As an antidote to stuffy indoor living, we should develop

gardens which encourage us to eat, work, play and rest out of doors. We need spots where we can escape from the extreme heat on sunny days, enclosed arbours where we are protected from the wind, conservatories where we can enjoy the winter sunshine, and verandas where we can shelter from the rain. In these settings we will be able to profit from the constantly changing climatic conditions, which act as a powerful metabolic stimulant. Our bodies contain a highly efficient temperature-regulating system, which is partly dependent on the vast network of tiny blood vessels in the skin. These arterioles have muscular walls which enable them to open or close as required, rather like the thermostat valves on a central heating radiator. When we need to lose heat, the arterioles dilate, bringing an increased flow of blood to the surface of the body for cooling. When body heat needs to be conserved, the vessels contract. Nowadays we live in indoor climates where the temperature is carefully controlled, and as a result the blood vessels become sluggish through lack of use. To keep them working at peak efficiency so that we can react quickly to changes in temperature, we should subject our body to occasional currents of cool air. This 'gymnastics for the arteries' can be achieved through wearing the lightest possible clothing when gardening or exercising out of doors.

When we are working indoors, the optimum temperature for comfort is several degrees higher than that for peak brain function. A cold shower can increase metabolism by 80 per cent, bringing a fresh flow of blood to the brain. Exposure to the wind has a similar effect: a gentle breeze of just 5 m.p.h. cools the body by a third or more, which empties the vast reservoirs of blood within the skin and increases the circulation to the heart and brain and other vital organs. This can provide a vigorous boost to mental activity, which is why we often think better, and are more creative, when we are exposed to the fresh air.

To get our brains in gear, the first thing we need to do is to leave an overheated room, step into a garden and take a deep breath. We should fill our lungs to the full with oxygen, for this is the fuel on which our lives depend. The Romans recognized this when they used the one word *spiritus* to describe both 'breath' and 'life force': when we absorb this energy we are 'inspired', and when we lose it we 'expire'. To drive this point home, try using the visualization trick devised by the poet Ella Wheeler Wilcox. As you breathe in, mentally recite the words 'Life . . . life . . . life', and conjure up a picture of what is taking place within your body. In your mind's eye, follow the journey the oxygen molecules take as they are drawn into the lungs, then absorbed by the red blood cells and transported to every cell in the body, where they bring vitality and regeneration. Too many people are habitual shallow-breathers. When we are sedentary we use little more than one tenth of our total lung capacity. In order to keep our chests working at peak efficiency, from time to time we need to put our lungs to full use. Surveys show that the most accurate predictor of someone's future health is the vital capacity of their lungs. This bellows power is enhanced by gardening, as it is by other forms of gentle aerobic exercise.

ROOM FOR COMPLAINT

THE MORE TIME WE SPEND IN A HEALTHY, OUTDOOR ENVIRONMENT, the less time we spend indoors in rooms which are often too hot, too dry and overladen with chemical fumes. More than three-quarters of London office workers complain of the stuffiness or staleness of the air in which they work. This makes them feel tired and irritable by the end of their working day. One likely cause of this discomfort is a low level of relative humidity. We function best in air which has a relative humidity of 45–55 per cent. In centrally heated rooms the humidity is often as low as 4 per cent, which is much dryer than the air in Death Valley or the Sahara Desert. In these parched conditions plants wilt, furniture shrinks, pianos go out of tune, eyes itch, skin becomes dry and leathery and fingernails break.

Closed rooms can also generate unhealthy patterns of air ionization. The outside air is teeming with electrically charged particles, which arise as a result of storms, the bombardment of cosmic rays, the transmission of ultraviolet light and the constant frictional movement of water, wind and soil. When we breathe, we draw these particles into our lungs. From here they are carried around the body, where they affect the cellular uptake of oxygen. Particles which carry a positive charge tend to reduce the tissue uptake, whereas those which bear a negative charge have the opposite, invigorating action. This effect is far from negligible. Tests show that when subjects are placed in atmospheres with a high level of positive ions, their eyes smart, their heads feel stuffy and they start to show symptoms of lethargy and lowered spirits. Put them in an atmosphere charged with negative ions and they quickly perk up and begin to feel alert and energetic. This explains some of the lethargy we feel in stuffy rooms, for there may be ten thousand negative ions in every cubic centimetre of pure mountain air, but only two hundred in polluted city streets and as few as twenty in enclosed homes and offices. This is a major problem for *Homo encapsularis*, as Dr Albert Kreuger, Professor of Bacteriology at the University of California, has warned: 'People travelling to work in polluted air, spending hours in urban dwellings, inescapably breathe ion-depleted air for substantial portions of their lives. There is increasing evidence that this ion-depletion leads to discomfort, enervation and lassitude, and loss of mental and physical efficiency.'

But the problems do not end here. Somewhere between 30 and 60 per cent of homes in Europe and America use gas as a fuel for cookers, water heaters and central heating boilers. If these appliances are not properly vented, they can generate dangerous levels of nitrogen dioxide, which can damage the lungs and increase the risk of wheezing, shortness of breath and asthma. Add to this the problem of mites, which love the warmth of modern buildings and find fitted carpets an ideal breeding ground. At one time asthmatics were advised to stay indoors to reduce their exposure to plant and grass pollens. Now they are often encouraged to spend as much time as possible out of doors, in order to reduce their contact with the dreaded house mite. Then there is the peril of background radiation. Most people believe that the main sources of environmental radiation are nuclear weapons, nuclear power stations and X-ray machines, but nearly half of all the radiation our bodies receive comes from radon, the naturally occurring radioactive gas which is constantly being released from the earth. We breathe this gas every day of our lives, but poorly ventilated rooms can double our exposure to it. There are things we can do to offset all these problems: we can install humidifiers and negative ion machines, fumigate rooms to exterminate the house mite, switch from gas to electricity and move to areas with low levels of radon. On the other hand, it is simpler by far to open the windows or to spend more time out of doors.

Fresh air will also alleviate the symptoms of Sick Building Syndrome, a recently identified menace which the World Health Authority believes may affect nearly a third of all new and recently remodelled buildings. This syndrome, which occurs when buildings are excessively insulated and have low rates of air exchange, gives rise to headaches, tiredness, irritability, poor concentration, and soreness and irritation of the eyes, nose and throat, symptoms which quickly clear when sufferers go outside. Some blame this malaise on the gas released from the widely used formaldehyde insulation foams, while others point the finger at the fluids used in photocopying machines or the fungi which grow under carpets, on walls and in the recesses of ventilation systems. The suspects are endless. Researchers at Harvard University have so far studied more than fifty possible air pollutants, incorporated in building materials, furnishings, fabrics, toiletries, cosmetics, cleaning materials and fly sprays. The only general conclusion they have reached is that breathing the tainted air of our own homes is more likely to cause cancer than breathing the polluted outdoor air of our cities.

The message is clear. We must take steps to improve the quality of our indoor air, but most importantly we must be prepared to spend more time out of doors. Our gardens need to be far more than places where we cultivate roses and raise rhubarb. They must in future become outdoor living rooms, where we are happy to spend a large part of our leisure time.

In parallel with this major lifestyle change, we should take the additional precaution of adorning our offices and homes with ferns and potted plants as a protection against Sick Building Syndrome. The value of this simple measure was demonstrated by a team of American space scientists, led by Dr Bill Wolverton. The NASA researchers introduced traces of three of the most common indoor pollutants – benzene, formaldehyde and trichloroethylene – into a series of sealed containers. Some of the containers were set aside to act as controls, while the others were furnished with a variety of potted plants, to see what effect they had on the quality of the enclosed air. After a lapse of twenty-four hours the air was analysed. The results showed that during this brief time the plants had acted as highly efficient scavengers, removing at least half the concentration of potentially carcinogenic pollutants. The most effective of the plant detoxifiers were English ivy, the peace lily and the gerbera.

LET THERE BE LIGHT

WORKING OUT OF DOORS BRINGS US BOTH THE BENEFITS OF FRESH air and the stimulus of exposure to the sun's rays. Fifty years ago the medical profession gave a great boost to the Nature Cure movement when it embarked on a vigorous campaign to encourage people to quit their gloomy city homes and bare their bodies to the sun. Nowadays the opposite advice is given with equal vehemence: we should stay out of the sun for fear of contracting skin cancer. The truth undoubtedly lies somewhere between these two extremes. For our health's sake we should avoid blistering, burning and extreme tanning, but should seek out the benefits of gentle and regular exposure to the sun's rays.

Herodotus, the first-century Greek physician, earned the title of the Father of Heliotherapy because of his enthusiasm for sun-bathing. 'Exposure to the sun is highly necessary in persons whose health needs restoring,' he wrote. This view, generally accepted throughout the pre-scientific age, gained further support at the beginning of the twentieth century, when investigations were made into the physiological effects of solar radiation. Ultraviolet light was discovered to be a powerful antiseptic and was used to disinfect wounds, purify water, and sterilize the casings of the early US space missiles so that they wouldn't contaminate the moon with the earth's germs. When we cough and sneeze we spread germs, but tests show that these are quickly destroyed by the sun's rays. This explains why respiratory diseases, coughs and colds are most easily transmitted indoors, which has earned them the French nickname *les maladies de l'ombre*, the diseases of darkness. Research has also revealed that exposure to the sun's rays stimulates the formation within the skin of Vitamin D, the sunshine vitamin which plays an essential role in building up healthy bones. Nowadays many people lose bone density as they age, a deterioration which is more closely associated with a lack of sunlight than with a dietary deficiency of vitamin D. Window glass obscures practically all the sun's ultraviolet rays, so the skin is able to manufacture vitamin D only when we are out of doors. Tests show that optimum levels of Vitamin D could be maintained if we exposed our face and legs to the sun for one or two hours per day.

Daylight also acts as a metabolic stimulant, increasing the output of the pituitary gland and speeding the formation of sex hormones. Zoologists find that animals in captivity fare much better, and breed more freely, when they are bathed in natural rather than artificial light. Some of the animals kept indoors at London Zoo became excessively sluggish, but perked up when their cages were fitted with special lamps which emitted ultra-violet light. Under this more natural lighting they were reported to be livelier and more interested in sex.

Daylight deprivation has a similar effect on human behaviour. Eskimos often sink into a state of depression and lethargy during the long winter months, a condition known as *perlerorneq* or Lapp sickness. This depression and ennui – now referred to as Seasonal Affective Disorder – is thought to be related to a drop in hormone levels and it can be cured by exposure to the light, a tonic guaranteed to lift our spirits and lower our stress levels. Professor Hans Selye, the founder of the International Institute of Stress in Montreal, made personal use of solar therapy and found it uniquely relaxing. He aimed to spend a few hours a day basking in the sun. 'I find this does me more good than any medicine,' he reported in his auto-biography, *The Stress of My Life*. 'My blood pressure is always several points lower after a relaxing sunbath.'

Solar therapy is not a modern invention. Excavations carried out at the Temple of Aesculapius in Epidaurus have revealed the remains of a long, south-facing gallery which opened from the temple's main sickroom. The ancient Greeks almost certainly used this as a sun terrace, where sick and convalescent patients could go to regain their health.

The Orthodox Jewish tradition also respects the benefits of fresh air. In the autumn, when the harvest is gathered in, the delightful custom of Succoth is celebrated with an eight-day festival during which rich and poor families alike take their meals out of doors in a primitive booth or *succah*. These booths are gaily decorated inside with flowers and fruit, and loosely covered with branches that leave a clear view of the stars above. The huts are crude because they are intended to recall the temporary dwellings that the children of Israel built on their forty-day journey through the wilderness. During the festival of Succoth, Jewish families escape the sophistication of modern life and re-establish their links with nature, giving thanks for the bounties of the earth in the *Hoshanah Rabbah*, or Great Hosanna.

Some Aquarian Age hippies have adopted a remarkably similar practice. They have satisfied their longing for a more natural, outdoor lifestyle by setting up homes in yurts. These dome-shaped houses, made from a framework of curved tree branches covered with a roof of felt, are the traditional dwellings of the nomadic people of Central Asia. Although they provide only the most primitive accommodation, with little more than sixteen feet of living space, the yurts keep people in touch with the elements, and induce what the Travellers claim is 'a very calm and happy feeling'. Few of us may wish to give up our home comforts and take to living permanently in primitive tents and huts, but we could all benefit from the metabolic stimulus of closer contact with the fresh air, wind, light and sun's rays. This is a tonic we automatically receive whenever we find time to enjoy the amenities of a Soul Garden.

The rapid urbanization of our western societies has provoked many profound changes of lifestyle, some of which threaten our health. Government campaigns have made us conscious of the risks of overeating, taking insufficient exercise and suffering too much stress, but many people remain unaware of the potential hazard of spending too much time in an uncongenial indoor environment. This can give rise to a cluster of symptoms – headache, tiredness, irritability and poor concentration – which are often referred to as Sick Building Syndrome. Scientists are struggling to find the cause, or causes, of this malady. While they do so, we would be well advised to find our own solution to the problem by spending more time in the open air.

The fastest growing activities today are those which take people into the great outdoors; pursuits such as backpacking, camping, caravaning, fishing, sailing and skiing. A Soul Garden is designed to foster this trend by providing facilities for alfresco eating, recreation, rest, work and play.

CHAPTER NINE

A Step in the Right Direction

'And they heard the voice of the
Lord God walking in the garden
in the cool of the day.'

GENESIS III, 8

*W*HAT IS THE STARTING POINT OF GARDEN DESIGN? DOES the structure of a garden dictate how it will be used, or should we begin with a clear idea of a garden's function and then work backwards to create the most appropriate layout? This is a matter of fundamental importance, for no two gardens are identical and no two gardeners have the same requirements, tastes and lifestyle. A garden achieves its full potential only when it takes account of the interrelated elements of structure and function.

If you have acquired a house with a ready-made garden, you will almost certainly need to adapt it to meet your personal requirements. If you haven't yet made any changes, you can be fairly sure that it's failing to give you of its best. In the same way, if you have a garden which serves a solitary purpose – providing a playground for the children, a place to sit on sunny days or an allotment for growing runner beans – you can be certain that you are nursing a grossly under-utilized asset.

Before we make any radical changes, there are some questions we need to ask. In the many articles and television programmes on gardening, which are exceedingly good at answering 'How to' queries, there is a surprising dearth of material on the more fundamental issues of 'Why?' and 'For what purpose?' They are strong on methodology but weak on theory. A gardening feature may tell us how to build a cold frame or grow cucumbers from seeds, but it will not consider the essential purpose of gardening. Why should we spend time in a garden – raising broad beans or edging a lawn – when we could be watching television or enjoying a convivial evening with friends? This is a question which needs to be addressed.

One way to get a fresh perspective on our contemporary approach to gardening is to delve again into the annals of horticultural history. The gardening priorities of the past can be a rich source of ideas which we can adapt to our own ends. Medieval monks used gardens primarily as sources of food and medicinal herbs, and kept stew ponds to provide them with a ready supply of fish during the lean winter months. We store our reserve supplies of fish in the freezer so we have no need of stew ponds, but we could make splendid use of a well-stocked herb garden. Seventeenth-century merchants kept secluded town gardens where they could hold trysts with their paramours. If that is our fancy today, then we must turn our gardens into similar shady hideaways with locked gates and secluded pavilions, accessible only via a tortuous pathway or maze so that we have advance warning of intruders. The European aristocracy of a slightly later date chose to flaunt their wealth in the garden. If we want to follow their example and create horticultural status symbols we will opt for modern sculptures, a gymnasium, a swimming pool and helicopter pad on the front lawn.

While garden fashions like these come and go, some features remain remarkably consistent, which suggests that they may be of particular significance. The garden alley, or promenade, is one such enduring theme. Ancient Greek houses were normally surrounded by walled gardens with colonnades around their perimeter so that people could walk in the shade. Similar colonnades were constructed around the public buildings of the day, the baths, academies and lyceums where people strolled while listening to the deliberations of poets and philosophers. Most monasteries had cloistered walks where monks would read, meditate and recite their prayers. Cities and fortified castles had rampart walks which followed the course of the turreted battlements, so that the inhabitants could saunter in the open air even when the city was under siege. When wealthy landowners began to create parkland estates, they festooned them with alleys and walkways. Towards the end of the sixteenth century, Squire Kirke of Cookeridge in Yorkshire planted 120 acres of woodland intersected by a network of walks in the form of a spider's web. At its hub was a clearing from which emanated twelve straight walks set like the spokes of a wheel and christened 'Jack and his eleven brothers'. These radial paths were criss-crossed with numerous circumferential paths, so that an endless variety of forest walks could be taken. This same layout – of central *rond-point* and radiating alleys – was later adopted by the town planners of Napoleon III, most noticeably in the roads leading to the Place de l'Étoile in Paris.

STEPPING OUT

AT THE START OF THE INDUSTRIAL AGE PUBLIC PARKS WERE BUILT SO that people could maintain their contact with nature by taking regular strolls in the open air. This was considered such a vital function that the first parks in England were known as 'public walks'. The paths running through these parks were made wide enough to permit the two-way traffic of elegant ladies showing off their crinolines, and at the weekends it became the vogue to use these broad walks as places of genteel exercise and extravagant fashion display. In France, the fashion for public walks led to the creation of numerous elegant 'boulevards', the word itself derived from the 'bulwarks' which provided the setting for earlier Parisian promenades.

Nowadays, because of limited space, few people think of their gardens as places for taking regular walks, yet this was once believed to be one of their main functions. Francis Bacon wrote his essay 'Of Gardens', not as a historical record of the gardens of his day, but to promote his personal vision of how an ideal garden should be constructed. His utopian garden was to include a series of alleys lined with hedges to provide shaded walks in summer and sheltered paths in winter, so that people could maintain their health by taking round-the-year outdoor exercise. However small the garden, it had to provide space for a walk, even if it was a circuit of only a few feet. The French developed the concept of the *bouver*, a short covered alley bedecked with honeysuckle, jasmine or scented clematis supported on a light wooden framework. Sometimes, when space was short, ingenious tricks were employed to make garden walks seem longer and more interesting. A favourite device in the days of Henry VIII was to construct spiral walks which twisted up and down the sides of large artificial mounds; King Henry had such a hump built at Hampton Court on a foundation created from a quarter of a million bricks. Not many of us are able to build on such a scale. However, if there is a will to take a garden walk, a way can always be found.

If you live in a town flat and have no access to a garden, plan a walk which takes you round a local park and adopt this as your garden path. For forty years I spent the week in a flat near Marble Arch, where there was no space for walking or even sitting out of doors. So, from the day I moved in, I adopted Hyde Park and Kensington Gardens as my personal 'back yard'.

In this way I had most of the pleasures, and few of the pains, of gardening. My appointed walk led me round the Serpentine, where I could take my morning constitutional, feed the ducks, watch the changing of the seasons, have a picnic supper or sit and read my evening paper. Now, in my retirement, I am creating what I hope and expect will be my final garden. This will contain a promenade, and my intention is that it will provide as much interest as my London walk. It starts with a scented *bouver* built on a living archway of willows, and follows an undulating course along steps and pathways to take in vistas and objects of interest and nostalgic significance. Part of the walk is gravelled so that it will remain dry even when it rains. This was the normal practice in eighteenth-century Britain, to make sure that promenades could be taken throughout the year; today it is often easier, and aesthetically more pleasing, to create weatherproof paths with bark chippings.

TRAIL SETTING

IF YOU DECIDE TO BUILD A GARDEN PATH, CONSIDER MAKING IT irregular rather than straight, for this will add greatly to its beauty and interest. A straight line may be the shortest distance between two points, but it is rarely the most attractive. Natural paths are never straight, partly because they follow the lie of the land, and also because we rarely walk in a dead straight line. Sinuous paths offer variety, and provide the surprise pleasure of turning a bend and coming face to face with an unexpected vista. The undulations also observe the aesthetic principles of the painter William Hogarth, who held that the 'line of beauty' should be curved to reflect the contours of the female figure. (I have modified a garden door to include a fascia board which directly follows Hogarth's axiom, since its scalloped outline is a direct copy of the silhouette of a reclining Renoir nude!) From a practical point of view the curves should be kept gentle, so that they retain a natural look, permit the easy passage of wheelbarrows and other such paraphernalia, and do not break the rhythm of one's walking step.

In essence, garden paths should be planned like a well-crafted novel, so that they offer a captivating beginning, an attention-holding middle and a satisfying conclusion. The start of the path should make a definite impact, so that users are aware that they are about to embark on a significant journey. The common devices used in the past to signal the beginning of a romantic garden walk were a door or gateway, a flight of steps, a narrow archway or a leafy tunnel. Such features immediately introduce an element of romance, mystery and magic, for doors and arches have always been used as symbolic markers at the start of a rite of passage. When we walk under a wedding archway, for example, we make a ceremonial gesture which shows that we are leaving behind our single lives and acquiring a new status. A similar feeling should be created the moment we step into a Soul Garden, when we symbolically leave behind our workaday cares and enter a world of romance, peace and rest.

The garden designed by Sir Edwin Lutyens at Castle Drogo in Devon succeeds in creating this transitional impact. It starts in dramatic fashion, with a tunnel of beech trees and then a flight of steps which visitors must negotiate before they can view the remainder of the garden. Passing through this tunnel stimulates a sense of anticipation and sets the atmosphere for the remainder of the tour. Dr Dougal Swinscow, whose delightful book *The Mystic Garden* expresses not only his love of gardening but also his Taoist philosophy and Christian faith, tells of the impact made by the start of the Castle Drogo walk: 'In the semi-darkness our everyday world is blacked out, our thoughts are stilled, our expectancy heightened. We go through a gate, step forward a couple of paces, and there suddenly the garden is displayed all around, a *coup de théâtre*.'

A similar effect is created in the gardens of Rousham in Oxfordshire. Here William Kent built a tunnel of trees and shrubs which gradually becomes less dense so that it offers tantalizing glimpses of the statues, stone walls and ponds which lie ahead. Walking through such a tunnel is rich in archetypal symbolism, since it suggests the figurative transition from darkness into light. When we pass through an arboreal tunnel, or even a short *bouver*, we are provided with the subconscious reassurance that however grim our lives may be there is always hope for a brighter future, and the constant promise of renewal.

POINTS OF INTEREST

AFTER BEGINNING OUR PATH WITH AN ARRESTING FEATURE – EVEN if it's simply a garden gate or a rose-covered archway – we then need to create an interesting, scenic route. This the great landscape designers of the past did with enormous flare. We may not have the same resources at our disposal, whether it be of time, space or money, but we can certainly benefit from their expertise. Every great garden, large or small, is designed to provide views varying from broad prospects to narrow vistas and tiny, peek-a-boo glimpses through *clairs-voyées* or grilles in walls. The grand landscape gardens offer panoramic vistas of wooded hills, bridges, statues, lakes and Grecian temples. Our surprise views will almost certainly not be on the same scale. They may reveal no more than a concealed garden seat nestling in an arbour of clipped yew hedging, a dovecote, a small lily pond, a bird bath, a sundial or a garden house hidden behind a boscage of evergreen shrubs. Nevertheless they serve the same function as the eighteenth-century obelisks and pavilions, in that they provide visual surprises and lures to lead the walker onwards.

Another way to enliven a garden walk is to make use of different paving surfaces such as cobblestones, patterned bricks or crazy paving infilled with heather and thyme. Variety is the spice of garden design. Batty Langley, the landscape gardener employed by the Duke of Kent in the early eighteenth century, used grottoes, sundials, fishponds and fountains to provide a non-stop display of harmonious objects 'that will present new and delightful Scenes to our View at every Step'. That principle should be followed, if only in scaled-down form, in every Soul Garden. With points of interest like these, strung like pearls along the walk, your feet will follow where your eyes are drawn.

Some of these features should trigger pleasant memories and reflections. We fill our homes with personal mementoes, family photographs and souvenirs from favourite holidays. What stops us from making similar use of our gardens? Trees can be planted when children are born, family initials worked into stone patios, and borders filled with plants and shrubs obtained as gifts from friends. My present garden covers little more than half an acre, but it would take more than forty minutes to cover the promenade if proper thought were given to all the objects on the way, many of which evoke significant memories or have symbolic meanings. In the near future I intend to fix descriptive labels to some of these features, and place appropriate mottoes beside others, to act as a stimulus to thought. Peter the Great did something very similar in the gardens of Peterhof, his palace on the shores of the Baltic Sea. He dotted the grounds with hollow lead statues, each of which represented a figure from one of Aesop's moral fables. Then, to make sure that neither he nor his guests would miss the educative value of the statues, he had them flagged with posts carrying a description of the characters and the moral messages they portrayed. Similar homilies were posted in many Renaissance gardens: for instance, 'All things are directed from the good to the good. Rejoicing in the present you must not prize wealth or desire dignity. Flee excess, flee affairs, rejoicing in the present.'

A more macabre message was embodied in the garden at Tyrers, an eighteenth-century property set on the wooded out-skirts of Dorking in Surrey. This contained a walk through the Valley of the Shadow of Death, adorned with coffin, skulls and moral epitaphs, all designed to provide a reminder of the vanity of man and the brevity of his life. Many modern gardens carry memorials to departed loved ones. The garden of designer David Hicks bears a portrait plaque of Lady Mountbatten, his mother-in-law, surrounded by shells which she herself had collected on her travels. Garden designer and historian Marc Schoellen has created a beautiful garden around his Luxembourg home which is filled with items of personal significance. The garden has a number of inviting walks, decorated with hornbeam hedges, wild-flower meadows, ponds, a shell-encrusted grotto and tempting vistas, and his advice to visitors is always: 'Let the paths lead you.' But the garden remains intensely personal, for at one point there is a gap which marks the exact spot where the sun sets on his birthday, and another opening which offers a view across the valley to St Peter's Church, the burial place of his father who co-designed the garden.

If you haven't access to a garden of your own at present, you might enjoy following an established nature trail in a public garden, as these provide both healthy outdoor exercise and instruction in natural history. The first nature trail was built by Claude François Denecourt, a wounded soldier who returned a cripple from Napoleon's campaigns to make his home in the Forest of Fontainebleau. Here he created a series of ten-kilometre promenades filled with intriguing diversions including a Druid's cavern, a grotto where village maidens were said to have hidden from a troop of lusty Cossacks, Charlemagne's venerable oak tree and a romantic forest glade which was claimed to be the trysting place of a chevalier and a totally fictitious 'Queen Nemerosa'. The lesson to be learned from the success of Denecourt's promenades, which were patronized by such eminent people as George Sand, Voltaire, Victor Hugo and Charles Baudelaire, is that garden walks and forest trails must be provided with entertaining features if they are to retain our interest.

Intrepid gardeners might even care to enliven their garden walks with an element of danger, a trick employed by an earlier generation of landscape designers. Gardens can be turned into adventure playgrounds or miniature assault courses by adding a rope walk or a see-saw bridge across a pond, providing this doesn't put children and elderly people at risk. This adds an element of excitement to the walk, clears the cobwebs from the mind and sets the adrenaline flowing. Edmund Burke, the eighteenth-century British statesman and author, firmly believed that anything that threatens our security can be a pathway to the sublime – a theory which inspired Sir Richard Hill to create a truly terrifying ten-mile walk around his garden at Hawkstone in Shropshire. This embraced a hazardous alpine bridge suspended across a rocky ravine and an ascent through a pitch-black tunnel which opened into a glowing grotto where a tall hermit waving a magic wand would suddenly appear and greet visitors in a gruff voice. (This was actually an articulated wax model operated by one of Sir Richard's gardeners.) But the greatest terror was saved till last, for when visitors left the grotto they found themselves perched on the Raven's Shelf, a narrow ledge jutting out perilously from the side of a cliff with a sheer rocky fall of several hundred feet below. This was the horticultural equivalent of a fairground ride on the Big Dipper. Few today can garden on such a grandiose scale, but we could all benefit from following Sir Richard's example and setting out to make our gardens places not only of beauty but also of excitement and fun.

GOING WITH THE FLOW

PATHS ARE MADE FOR FREE AND EASY CIRCULATION AROUND A garden; but don't be surprised if you show a preference for walking in one particular direction. It's an odd fact that when we are sedentary we tend to circulate objects in a clockwise direction, as we do when dealing cards. But when we're on the move we invariably opt to go in the opposite direction. When joggers enter a public park they can turn either to the right or to the left, but in practice they nearly always choose to make an anti-clockwise circuit, as I've noted both in London and in New York. Most race tracks follow an anti-clockwise course, which is also the direction traditionally taken on the dance floor. Whirling dervishes turn that way and so, too, do baseball players when they head for first base. Sacred processions around Celtic shrines follow that route, as do the ceremonial circuits around Christian churches. Even the bathwater in the northern hemisphere rotates in this direction when the plug is pulled, due to the rotation of the earth. So if you have a choice, plan your garden path so that it goes with the flow and follows a widdershins direction. If this becomes boring, try walking backwards to get a change of scenery! One Chippewa Indian from Minnesota has taken to doing this wherever he goes, and claims that the back-to-face walking has cured his backache, eased the arthritis in his knees, made him feel younger and deep-ened his spiritual life. There was a tradition among his Sioux brothers, he said, of doing things backwards 'to make people laugh and forget about their problems . . . trusting the Great Spirit to catch them if they fell'.

The design of garden paths is important, but more important still is the way those paths are used. However well stocked they may be with visual delights and mementoes, they must be regularly enjoyed if they are to be of lasting therapeutic benefit.

FORWARD MARCH

OUR LIVES TODAY ARE BECOMING INCREASINGLY SEDENTARY. A large part of our time is spent sitting in chairs, watching television, operating computers and driving cars. 'Why do you think God gave us two legs?' a mother asked her daughter. 'One is for the clutch, the other for the accelerator,' was the immediate response. But it isn't just a joke: our inactivity is having an adverse effect on our health.

Many of the chronic ailments we suffer today – obesity, varicose veins, coronary disease, chronic fatigue, depression, back pain and muscular rheumatism – are related in part to lack of exercise. This is why they are sometimes called the 'hypokinetic diseases', the diseases caused by inactivity. One simple solution is to find more time for brisk walking, and what better place to get this exercise than in one's own back yard? This is the perfect way to keep slim, for a half hour's walk burns up about three hundred calories, which if taken on a daily basis should result in the loss of over a stone of surplus flab a year. (The scales may not record the same weight loss because the additional exercise will lead to the build-up of lean muscle tissue, which is considerably heavier than the fat it replaces.) The extra walking will also provide an excellent metabolic stimulus. At rest we use only a small percentage of the body's 60,000-mile circuit of blood vessels. When we start to exercise – hoeing the garden or walking round a park – there can be a fifty-fold increase in the size of the vascular field, which means that far more life-giving blood is flowing around the body. The additional exercise will also reduce the level of cholesterol in the blood, strengthen the heart muscles and lessen the risk of coronary disease.

A prolonged survey of nine thousand British civil servants revealed that cardiac health depends far more on daily levels of walking than on occasional bouts of jogging, tennis and squash. Heart irregularities, for instance, were found to be 50 per cent more frequent in men whose lifestyles involved little daily walking than in those who walked for twenty minutes or more per day. If your garden is small, you may need to supplement the walking with a little more digging, weeding, raking and hoeing to get the necessary level of aerobic exercise. Or you could turn the garden into a circuit-training course: hopping along the path, fifty skips on the patio, press-ups on the garden seat, running five times up and down the steps, twenty semi-squats on the lawn, and then twelve chin-ups on a trapeze hanging from a convenient tree.

By taking this regular outdoor exercise you'll certainly enhance the quality of your life, and may even increase its length. One centenarian claimed that he owed his longevity to the wedding-day bargain he made with his wife. They had agreed that whenever they had an argument, the one who was found to be in the wrong would take a long penitential walk round the garden. 'As a result,' he said, 'I've spent a large part of my life taking exercise in the open air.'

THE TRAMP'S PHILOSOPHY

TAKING A GARDEN STROLL CAN ALSO HELP TO STILL THE MIND. Whenever you're under pressure you'll find there's no better escape than to quit the scene of action and take a carefree walk in the great outdoors. This is what the Australian aborigines do when they feel oppressed by the demands and pressures of modern life. Instead of staying put and enduring the ceaseless stress of city life they pack their bags and go walkabout in the bush, thereby recapturing the freedom enjoyed by their nomadic ancestors. Many people have found this a perfect way of coping with mental strain, including the philosopher Kierkegaard, who said: 'Every day I walk myself into a state of well-being and walk away from every illness. I have walked myself into my best thoughts, and I know of no thought so burdensome that one cannot walk away from it.'

This is a splendid prophylactic exercise. Everyone who is fortunate enough to own a garden should make a point of walking around the grounds every day, rather as a contemplative monk might walk around the cloisters of an abbey. This is an ideal way to unwind after a period of prolonged stress. Charles Darwin was a workaholic who suffered from a wide variety of tension ailments, including muscular rheumatism and blinding headaches. He found that the easiest way to relax was by taking a stroll around the garden he created at Down House, his home in Kent. It was along a meandering walk between yew and box hedges, leading into a wood of densely planted wild cherries and birch trees, that he took his daily constitutional.

Scientific tests confirm that outdoor walking aids recovery from stress. In a typical experiment a group of volunteers was subjected to the artificial stress of performing a series of demanding mental tasks. Their rate of recovery was then measured under four different conditions: when they were reading, listening to music, walking in an urban area or walking in an area filled with vegetation and trees. The results showed that post-stress recovery was quickest when a relaxing, leafy walk was taken.

To achieve this tranquillizing effect, try to clear your mind of anxious thoughts and then take a slow walk around the garden, idly observing the sights and sounds and smells. Set no definite objectives or schedules. This is *your* time, to be spent in *your* way. Thoreau recommended strolling at the pace of a camel, which he said was the only animal which could walk and ruminate at the same time. Others have suggested a gentle saunter, a word itself derived from the leisurely, meditative pace the pilgrims took when they made their way to the holy land or 'Saint-Terre'. It is when we walk at this pace, in an untroubled, receptive frame of mind, that we are most likely to find the solution to our problems. 'Walking solves it' is an old recipe for nervous anxiety, and what was sometimes described as 'the tramp's philosophy' became a popular practice in Victorian times, when ladies were advised to create a flower garden surrounded by a small and simple walk where they could both exercise and think. The length of the path did not matter, they were assured in *The Ladies' Companion to the Flower Garden*, providing it was gentle and continuous. If they had space for only a pot of mint, the author said, they 'should surround this plot with an oval path' so they could keep up a gentle walking pace.

Inventors, philosophers and scientists often find it easier to think when they are on the move. A wild garden can be the perfect think-tank, an ideal setting for the unconscious processes of creative thought. Freud gave his early treatments while out for a stroll with his patients, not when they were lying on a couch. The idea for the steam engine came to James Watt when he was out walking. Nobel Prize winner Godfrey Hounsfield, co-inventor of the EMI scanner, reports that many of his brightest ideas come to him while he is ambling idly through the countryside. Academics today may work indoors, in laboratories and lecture halls, but their predecessors taught and thought outdoors – indeed, the very word 'academic' is derived from the garden of Academus where Plato held his classes. Not only the ancient Greeks but also a group of Chinese scholars, known as the Seven Sages of the Bamboo Grove, found their inspiration and acquired their understanding in garden settings.

It is often when we roam around a garden, relaxed in mind and in close touch with nature, that we gain our most meaningful spiritual insights. This is a form of contemplation very similar to the walking meditation of the Pure Land School of Buddhism. When our minds are calm and we travel without striving to reach a particular conclusion, every step can be an arrival. People will undertake long pilgrimages in search of the truth, but truth is universal and can be found as easily in a garden as in a distant shrine or holy place. 'Don't look for the path far away,' the *Tung-Ch'an* warns, 'the path exists under our feet.'

PUTTING THE GARDEN TO BED

THE BEST TIME TO TAKE THESE MEDITATIVE STROLLS IS IN THE COOL of the evening. Walking is an excellent prelude to sleep. (Tests show that the cadence of a mother's walk is the best rhythm for rocking babies to sleep.) Every evening before you retire to bed, make a habit of taking a final stroll around the garden so you can say goodnight to the birds and trees. If necessary, install a series of low-voltage garden lamps to light your way. When you take these nocturnal perambulations, free your conscious mind of all your concerns and preconceived ideas. You are not travelling to satisfy a need or achieve a particular goal, as you have been during the working day. Allow your mind to become a tabula rasa, a clean slate, on which your subconscious thought processes are free to write their own script. When you make your final rounds, put your mind on automatic pilot and let your senses take command. If you have stocked your garden with aromatic flowers and herbs you will find they smell more sweetly when the sun goes down and the air is moist. Sounds will also be heard more easily at night, when the light fades and the ears take over from the eyes. As the rumble and roar of the traffic lessens, you will be able to hear more clearly the gentle whisper of the wind rustling through the trees, magical sounds which our primitive forebears believed were made by revenants or ancestral spirits returning to their old haunts.

This is a time when gardeners should be both wanderers and wonderers. If the sky is clear we now have a chance to marvel at the majesty of the moon and stars. During the day our eyes are often so busy that they do not see the natural beauty which surrounds us, but at night, when we gain a brief respite from the constant distraction of whirring figures, words and signals, we can witness once again the unadorned marvels of the universe. This we must do with the wonderment of a child, as if we were viewing the world for the very first time. Just imagine how excited we would be if the stars made their appearance only once in a thousand years. Everybody then would rush out to see them, just as they do now to observe a total eclipse of the sun or a rare sighting of Halley's comet. Those stars which light our evening sky are a constant reminder of the permanence of nature; however ephemeral our own lives may be, when we see the Great Bear, the Plough and the Evening Star, we know those same stars shone down on Adam and Eve and will be throwing their light on our offspring until the end of time. When we have looked up and acknowledged their presence, we can retire to bed with the reassurance given by Robert Browning: 'God's in his heaven – All's right with the world!'

The writer Nigel Nicolson recalls that during the Second World War his family were separated by thousands of miles. To narrow the gap between them, they made a pledge that, wherever they were, they would look up at the same point in the heavens at midnight on the last day of every month and think of absent friends and family. They chose to look at the famous cluster of stars known as the Pleiades, because they are easy to find and have four particularly bright members, one for each of the Nicolson nuclear family. This is a custom we could well repeat, to strengthen our bonding with those we love.

When we take these nightly walks we cease to be isolated individuals and become once more a tiny but integral part of the cosmos. The Kalahari bushmen know this feeling well, and describe wholeness as 'walking again with the moon and stars'.

steppi

Gentle walking is one of the finest of all holistic exercises, for whereas weight-lifting develops the muscles and meditation stills the mind, walking acts as a tonic for body, mind and spirit. It was for many years part of the spiritual discipline of the medieval monks, who walked in contemplation around their monastery courtyards. It was also a source of enlightenment for the peripatetic Greek philosophers, who found that inspiration came most readily when they were on the move.

To obtain the full benefits, a Soul Garden must be used to promote regular outdoor activity. To encourage this use even the smallest of gardens should contain a walk, where regular strolls can be taken to enjoy the passing sights and sounds. An excellent time to take these reflective rambles is in the early evening, when scents and sounds are heightened and the glories of the evening sky are revealed. This makes a perfect relaxing end to a working day and provides an ideal preparation for a sound night's sleep.

CHAPTER TEN

A Man for All Seasons

'To everything there is a season, and a time to every purpose under the heaven: A time to be born, and a time to die.'

ECCLESIASTES III, 1–2

A gardener's life is never dull, for everything in a garden is in a constant state of flux. Even the tiniest shrub border responds to the changing seasons and the daily fluctuations in the weather. No two days, or even two moments of the same day, are exactly similar.

Nothing in the natural world is static, which is in sharp contradistinction to the urban world of metal, concrete, glass and stone. Unlike a tree, a towering office block looks much the same whatever the time of day or year, for round-the-clock neon lighting has turned night into day. Central heating and air conditioning have masked the distinction between summer and winter. This sameness eventually becomes tedious, for we need the stimulus of change; variety is the spice of life, uniformity the kiss of death.

Some of our current plethora of stress-related illnesses arise because we have lost our ability to adapt to change. Our lives have in many ways become too predictable for our own good. We need to develop the country dweller's ability to live with uncertainty and ambiguity, for the more we vary our lives, the more we strengthen our powers of adaptation. During the week we may be tied to a strict routine, but in a garden during our leisure hours we can do things as we please. If the fancy takes us we can get up early and watch the approach of the dawn. We can walk barefoot over the lawn or sleep in a hammock under the stars. To increase our ability to cope with change, we must seek it out. To become flexible, we must practise flexibility.

Our forebears did not expect to be able to exercise rigid control over their daily lives. Their existences were governed by nature rather than machines, and time was judged not by the clock but by the rising and setting of the sun. They had no diaries of tightly scheduled appointments. They were opportunists who made the most of what nature had to offer. Compared with that of a medieval farmer, our lives today show a remarkable sameness and homogeneity. One five-star hotel is very much like another, whether it is in Rotterdam or Rangoon. The view from an office window – of pavements, streets and apartment blocks – looks very similar whatever the time of year. This is not so in the countryside, or in a well-stocked city garden, where everything is subject to constant change.

Nowadays, one of the reasons we take holidays is because we need a break from our stultifying daily routine. For gardeners every day can become a holiday, especially if the garden is planted so that it gives plenty of seasonal variety. That's why it's never wise to specialize in a single crop. A garden is for every day of the year, and something is amiss if you have to tell your friends, 'You should have come last month when the rhodo-dendrons were in bloom.' Gardens can be planned so that they echo the changing seasons – the ancient Greeks made Vertumnus the god of both gardens and the seasons – and there are numerous gardening books which provide a month-by-month guide to flower displays. Snowdrops can be planted to welcome the New Year. Daffodils, narcissi and aconites are the harbingers of spring. Forsythias bloom in March, magnolias and cherry trees in April and azaleas and laburnums in May. During the summer the choice of colourful flowers is endless, and in the autumn it's possible to enjoy the gloriously rich tones of maples and Virginia creepers. In winter, pleasure can be taken from the winter-flowering viburnums, jasmine and heathers. In this way the garden can be stocked to provide endless seasonal variation, so there is always something of current interest and something to anticipate in the weeks ahead.

It is easy today to become obsessed with ephemeral crazes, fads and fashions. Every morning the newspapers offer us details of the latest political scandals, crime stories and global health warnings, news items which lose their impact almost before the ink is dry. This is not true of a garden, which can never be a passing vogue or momentary attraction. A garden is an ongoing pursuit, an interest which can never date and never stale.

Thoreau had no time for newspapers, claiming that nothing of note had happened in Europe since 1649, when Cromwell suppressed the uprising of the Levellers. He took delight in observing nature and noting the changing colours of the leaves in the fall, which roused in him 'a sort of autumnal madness'. When one of his friends asked him what he would do to keep himself amused when he retired to the isolation of Walden Pond, he replied: 'Will it not be employment enough to watch the seasons?' This is a non-stop entertainment which every garden can provide.

In Victorian times it was customary for middle-class families to keep a diary of the gardening year, often accompanied by watercolour sketches. In this journal a record was kept of when the first snowdrops appeared, the day trees and shrubs were planted, the day the first cuckoo was heard and the exact moment the house martins started their nest building and the hedgehog began its winter hibernation. This is a custom well worth reviving, not only because it increases our powers of observation but because it makes us more acutely conscious of the seasonal ebb and flow.

It was during this era – at the start of the scientific age – that educated people found pleasure in carrying out their own experiments. Many Victorians took a keen interest in the weather, installing rain gauges so they could keep a weekly tally of the rainfall. They watched the movements of wind vanes so they could note the direction of the prevailing wind, and hung thermometers on outside walls so they could record each day's maximum and minimum temperatures. Barometers, too, were in constant use. Every morning a check was made to see if the air pressure was rising or falling. Nowadays we take less personal interest in climate change and get whatever information we need from TV or radio weather forecasts. But however well we shield ourselves from the elements, our bodies are still extremely responsive to climatic change. The weather has a profound effect on our mood. On bright days our disposition is 'sunny'; on dull days we feel 'under a cloud'; on muggy days our spirits droop and we complain that we are 'under the weather'. Tests show that climatic factors also play a part in determining our behaviour, rate of growth, energy levels and resistance to infection. For the typical town dweller the weather is a constant source of conversation and complaint, because it is generally judged to be either too hot, too cold, too wet, too humid, too stormy or too dull. But to a gardener every variety of weather is welcome for the contribution it makes. The rain is needed to nourish the crops, the frost breaks up the soil and the high winds clear the trees of dead branches which may be out of the reach of pruning ladders.

To understand ourselves, we need to appreciate the changes which are taking place in the surrounding atmosphere. Few working people today can find the time to keep a daily log of rainfall, temperatures and wind speeds, but everyone would benefit from keeping a watchful eye on the barometer. Even small alterations in atmospheric pressure can have a profound effect on our bodily performance. A decrease of only 0.01 lbs per square inch lowers the pressure on our bodies by 28 lbs, which is enough of a difference for us to feel. When barometric pressure falls, the body tissues swell, which explains why so many people can foretell the approach of storms by the onset of headaches and rheumatic pain. When pressure rises we become slower in our reactions and more prone to accidents. This is a more serious hazard for motorists than fog and ice. A road accident study in Hamburg showed that while frost increased crashes by 5 per cent, the arrival of a high-pressure front caused road accidents to soar by 40 per cent. Sudden changes in air pressure can also have a dramatic effect on our risk of heart attacks, according to studies carried out by epidemiologist Professor Philippe Amouyel of Lille University, which show that a pressure rise of 10 millibars leads to an 11 per cent increase in heart attacks. It is obviously perilous for us to ignore these climatic changes. Rather than hide from the elements, we need to become more weatherwise.

THE CALM CENTRE

A SOUL GARDEN PROVIDES US WITH THE STIMULUS OF ENDLESS variety and change, but at the same time it offers us the security of consistency and permanence. Within a natural setting, things develop in a way which is orderly and wholly predictable. The sun is constantly on the move, but its progress is so consistent that we can tell the time by measuring the shadow it casts on a sundial. The seasons may come a little early or late, but we know with absolute certainty that the longer, lighter days of spring will always follow the dark days of winter, and we can be equally sure that, however disastrous the summer weather, there will rarely be an autumn when we won't have a profusion of fruit, nuts and vegetables. This must have been a source of enormous comfort to our ancestors, who would have longed to exchange the cruel cold of winter for the warmer summer months. Think how avidly they must have greeted the return of spring and the opportunity to sample fresh produce again, when there was no simple way of preserving food for the long winter period.

Throughout the world, the regular seasonal transitions of spring, summer, autumn and winter have been made the focal point of legends, feasts and festivals. They were once important landmarks in the social calendar, but have now been drained of most of their religious and mystical significance. In Britain the communal religious festivals gradually developed into trade fairs and commercial markets. Now they are mere bank holidays, a time for personal rest rather than community celebration.

Most people like to have a structure to their lives. We need to know where we stand in relation to the cosmic framework of time and space. The Neolithic people constructed elaborate stone henges so they could measure, and anticipate, the regular phases of the sun. The Druid priests could tell when it was midnight by the positioning of the stars. Nowadays we have lost these skills. Unable to tell the time without a watch or to find our way without a map and compass, we rely on tools to tell us where we are.

But we still have a need for fixed points of reference, to prevent us from being lost in the void. For the pious there have always been the constraints of the religious calendar. For Orthodox Jews, nearly every month has its appointed festival or feast day: Yom Kippur, Rosh Hashanah, the Passover, the Feast of Tabernacles, Succoth, Purim and Chanukah. The same is true of devout Christians, whose year revolves around the celebration of the saints' days and the devotional schedules of Advent, Epiphany, Lent, Easter, Whitsun and Trinity. For society folk in England there is the strict routine of the social calendar: Ascot, Henley, the Eton and Harrow match, Wimbledon, Cowes regatta, the Chelsea Flower Show and the Badminton Horse Trials. But what is there to give shape to other people's lives? All that remains for many is the working week and the nine-to-five daily grind, an unrelenting round which knows no seasonal variation whatsoever. No wonder so many people feel lost when they retire and lose the structure of their working years.

When we work in a garden we respond to a totally different rhythm. Here we learn to abandon our quest for certainty and perfection, for we know that in the real world everything is unstable, unpredictable and flawed. At the same time we gain the absolute assurance that while things may be in a constant state of flux, in the long run everything is stable, secure and enduring. In time a well-loved garden becomes an emotional foxhole into which we can retreat when the outside hurly-burly grows too fierce. Here we can find the still centre within the raging storm.

In a garden we learn tolerance. Whether we are growing vegetables or raising carnations we soon come to realize that we will never achieve perfection. We spend our time coping with leaf curl, mildew, cankers, grey mould, brown rot, die-back, blights and galls, and this makes it easier for us to tolerate the peccadilloes of our neighbours and friends. We become pragmatists, quite content to settle for acceptable outcomes rather than ideal solutions. In a garden nothing is perfectly regular, so why should we look for congruence in the remainder of our lives? Surveys show that our ideal of human beauty is one of perfect regularity of figure and face. But why should we expect the human animal to be symmetrical when the rest of nature is so wildly incongruous? In fact we are far more lopsided than we fondly imagine. In most people the right ear is lower than the left, and one eye larger and one side of the face more photogenic than the other. In men, the right testicle is normally larger than the left and slightly less pendant. In women the left breast is generally larger and lower than the right. If we could learn to love these eccentricities – just as we admire the asymmetry of a bonsai tree or ikebana flower arrangement – perhaps we'd be a trifle less anxious about our outward appearance and a little more inclined to accept our friends, 'warts and all'.

THE INNER CLOCK

WE HAVE LONG SINCE LEFT BEHIND OUR PASTORAL ORIGINS, BUT WE are still seasonal animals. This was recognized towards the middle of the nineteenth century when doctors began to take a close interest in what was then called geomedicine, the relationship between man and his environment. Now given the name of chronobiology, this subject is studied today with far greater scientific exactitude. We live in hermetically sealed homes and offices, and may feel that we are sheltered from the outside world. But in truth our bodies still respond to the rhythms of nature. All living organisms, from cabbages to kings, respond to the twenty-four-hour circadian cycle. Research has shown that the daily revolution of the earth affects our mood, hormonal output, memory, body temperature, sleep, pulse rate, blood sugar levels, powers of concentration and energy levels. Less apparent, but equally telling, are the biological changes which arise in response to the changes of the seasons. There are now known to be at least forty biological variables which fluctuate according to the time of year. Children raised in temperate climates put on weight in the winter, but they show the maximum gains in height during the spring and summer. This is no trivial effect, for the reported increase in weight during the winter can be as much as 100 per cent, and the summer increase in height of the order of 50 per cent. For no known reason, symptoms of peptic ulceration are at their highest in the spring and autumn in both England and America. Births are more common in the spring, which is also the most popular time for making wills, according to probate records dating back to the beginning of the twentieth century.

More so than we generally realize, our destinies are bound up with the rhythms of our natural environment. This was recognized by Hippocrates, long before the sciences of geomedicine and chronobiology were born. In his famous treatise *Airs, Waters, Places* the Father of Medicine wrote: 'Whosoever would study medicine aright – must consider the effect of the seasons of the year and the differences between them.' We do our bodies a disservice if we try to ignore these cosmic influences. Our health would benefit if we could live by the natural diurnal and seasonal rhythms, rather than by the clock and the appointment diary. This may be difficult to achieve during the working week, but when we are within the confines of a Soul Garden it becomes much easier to follow the lead of our innate body rhythms.

Primitive people observed and respected these fixed life cycles. Night followed day. Each month the moon passed through the same phrases. Every year seed time was followed by harvest. Time was measured, and courses set, by the regular movements of the stars. From these everyday observations our ancestors developed a cyclical view of time, an outlook which imbues a sense of permanence, order, leisureliness and hope. Gardeners inhabit the same world. They can foretell the changes which each season will bring. They know the time of year their flowers will break into bloom, and the order in which the fruit on their trees will mature in the autumn. For every living thing there is a time and a season. Nothing can be hurried, because everything has its place in the preordained sequence of events.

The timescale of civilized man is totally different. Since the invention of the chronometer, we have come to adopt a linear view of time. Our lives today are governed by the endless ticking of the clock. The ancients talked of the Wheel of Time, the constant circle of birth and rebirth. We choose a totally different metaphor: for us, life is a constantly flowing stream. In our mind's eye time marches or flies; it never stands still and it certainly never recedes. This linear view of time makes us harried and impatient, and is the root cause of the hurry sickness which has become such a destructive feature of our modern lives.

In a Soul Garden we can escape this harassment. Here we can dispense with watches and work to nature's rhythm rather than Greenwich Mean Time. Here we can follow the promptings of our biological clocks rather than obey the merciless dictates of the appointments diary. We can work when we feel energetic and rest when we are tired. Meals can be taken when we are hungry and sleep when we are fatigued, rather than at preordained times. If possible, we should also find some personal way of celebrating the passage of the seasons, so that we give a framework to the calendar year. We might decide, for instance, to hold a regular garden party to mark the summer solstice. In December the arrival of midwinter's day could be honoured by decking the house with holly and inviting friends in to enjoy a glass of steaming punch. On the first day of spring neighbours could be given posies of flowers fresh picked from the garden. The regular observance of these events will give continuity to your life and create the comforting feeling that both the future and the past are captured in the eternal present.

LAW AND ORDER

IN THIS WAY A SOUL GARDEN HELPS TO CONVEY A SENSE OF stability and order. We need to be reassured that the generative forces of nature will always transcend the destructive forces of man. During the Second World War, at the height of the blitz on London, a City church was preparing for its harvest festival service. A team of helpers gathered on the Saturday morning and set out a splendid display of flowers, fruit and vegetables around a central sheaf of corn. But the thanksgiving service was never held, for the church was totally destroyed in a bombing raid that night. For some months the building lay in ruins until, in the spring, when workmen were raking through the debris, they discovered that green shoots were springing up from the shattered altar steps. As the summer proceeded these shoots grew into a healthy clump of corn, a living testimony to the unconquerable regenerative powers of nature.

We need to be reminded constantly of this never-failing strength. Whatever we may do to damage the tropical rainforests or puncture the ozone layer, nature will always triumph over our folly. Gardeners know this to be true, and from practical experience will readily agree with Horace, the Roman poet, who said: 'Though you drive Nature out with a pitchfork, she will find her way back.'

A GROWTH AREA

A GARDEN IS A PLACE OF GROWTH, FOR PEOPLE AS WELL AS FOR plants. Every time we tackle fresh tasks, we develop new skills and enhance our feelings of competence and self-worth. To get the full benefit of a Soul Garden, it must be to some extent the product of our own efforts. In this respect we reap what we sow. When we design a garden we give expression to our personalities in a way which is far more revealing than our other forms of personal display. A garden is something we can create ourselves, which makes it far more an object of personal pride than an expensive suit or a flashy car.

One of the pyschological benefits of gardening is that it fully occupies the mind and displaces all our other worries. In a garden we can concentrate on a single activity in a way which is often impossible at other times, when we may be juggling with several different tasks and trying to cope with a non-stop succession of interruptions and distractions. A Zen Buddhist noviciate once asked his master to give him a definition of the *Tao* or Way. The master replied: 'When I am hungry, I eat. When I am tired, I sleep.' The student was perplexed by this nebulous answer. Wasn't this what everyone did? 'No,' said the master, 'most people are never totally in what they are doing, when eating they may be absent-mindedly preoccupied with a thousand different thoughts ... The supreme state of a thoroughly integrated person is to be without a divided mind.'

In a garden it is not difficult to find this calm focus. Everyone wants to feel needed, and a sense of purpose is an integral part of our concept of self-worth. Occasionally, when we are off colour, we may be content to be cared for by others, but most of the time we want to exercise our own nurturing instinct. This need can be met within even the tiniest garden plot. Bulbs can be grown in pots. Herbs can be cultivated from seeds planted in aluminium trays. Indoor greenhouses can be built in the darkest garage or basement, provided they are properly lit. (One simple solution is to erect two forty-watt fluorescent tubes connected to automatic timers so that they provide ten hours of darkness and fourteen hours of light.) If you have access to a roof garden, window box or outside courtyard, you can take up the ancient Oriental art of cultivating bonsai trees. This in itself will give you a chance to exercise your nurturing skills, for the trees will need daily watering in the summer, twice-yearly feeding with a liquid fertilizer, occasional repotting and regular pruning of top shoots and roots.

If time is short and you have no access to an outdoor space, try cultivating an indoor jungle garden in a glass terrarium. Obtain a large fish tank and cover it over with a sheet of glass. At the bottom of the tank place a layer of gravel covered with two or three inches of moist compost. Above this you are free to create a wondrous hothouse garden, with stones, lumps of wood and whatever exotic house plants take your fancy. Since the moisture is trapped within the container, the garden will not need watering more than every few months. The only other attention it will require is occasional pruning to remove dead leaves and flowers.

By caring for plants we develop the feminine side of our nature, the gentle, passive yin rather than the more aggressive, active yang. By tending, we learn tenderness. When we carry out delicate gardening tasks we find employment for our minds and also for our hands. It's a sobering thought that our finest acquisition – the human prehensile hand – is now falling into disuse. Today we use our fingers mainly to push buttons and operate keyboards, relatively coarse actions which pigeons can be trained to do with their beaks. We no longer do intricate needlework. We don't knit or carve wood. Even in the kitchen our hands are becoming increasingly redundant. Instead of peeling vegetables, we buy them from the supermarket ready prepared. We don't wash dishes, we put them in the dishwasher. Throughout all aspects of our lives, machines are performing the work which would previously have been done by hand. Yet manual work can be highly therapeutic. When we are tense we instinctively search for something to do with our hands. We draw doodles on scraps of paper, fiddle with paper clips, wring our hands, drum our fingers on the table, or handle calming stones and worry beads. Gardening is relaxing because it gives us something to do with our hands. Whether we are weeding, sowing, pruning or planting, gardening is essentially a 'hands on' job. This is maintenance in the original sense of the word, which stems from the French word *main*, meaning a hand. When we garden we are literally 'in touch' with nature. This contact is beneficial for both gardener and plant. Research work carried out at the Bolcani Institute in Israel has shown that the losses of vegetables which always arise when seedlings are moved from a greenhouse to an outside position can be reduced from 30 per cent to 5 per cent if they are stroked before they are transplanted.

CHARACTER BUILDING

GARDENING CAN BE A SOURCE OF CHARACTER TRANSFORMATION. Some people inject beauty into their lives by constructing a picturesque landscape garden. Many gain self-esteem from their gardening triumphs. For others gardening is a lesson in humbleness, simplicity or patience. We may get angry with people and irritated by things, but gardeners quickly learn that it's futile to get cross with shrubs which won't grow to the height stipulated in the catalogue. The more time we spend in a garden the more patient we become and the more we learn to co-operate with the inevitable. *Que sera, sera* becomes the gardener's watchword – 'what will be, will be'. We learn to be flexible and ready to seize whatever opportunities come our way. We don't expect certainties. We live a day at a time and take things as they come. We don't look forward to a better world, we're quite content to make the best of the one we have. We are not perfectionists. As gardeners we learn to take the good with the bad because we realize that there are no roses without thorns, and no flower beds without weeds.

In a garden we learn humility, partly because we understand that all living matter is made from the same raw ingredients. Everything is part of the cosmic whole, and even though its form and function may vary, it shares the same *élan vital*. We have no reason to consider ourselves the lords of creation. Our force is puny beside that of earthquakes, storms and tidal waves. A typical hurricane expends more energy in a minute than America uses in electricity in fifty years, according to a recent estimate. Given these facts, the reflective gardener can hardly harbour feelings of self-importance. Life, when viewed from this perspective, becomes exceedingly simple. We pass through a life cycle like that of the flowers and trees. We are born, we take nourishment, we reproduce, we interrelate with other living organisms, we serve our appointed function, we wither and finally we die. This is the destiny of every human being, whether rich or poor, male or female, black or white.

Gardeners are generally cheerful people. Their work gives them hope, even though they experience numerous setbacks and disappointments. Their gardens are the laboratories in which they work to create a better world. The novelist Vita Sackville-West is one of the many writers who have commented on this sanguine trait. 'The most noteworthy thing about gardeners is that they are always optimistic, always enterprising, and never satisfied. They always look forward to doing something better than they have ever done before,' she wrote. This positive outlook is of great benefit in preventing disease, in enabling us to cope with stress and in equipping us to recover from serious illness.

Our daily lives may give us cause to despair, but the moment we step into a garden our faith in the future is restored. When winter comes we know that spring is never far behind, and with it the perennial promise of new growth, new life, new hope.

COMPLETING THE JIGSAW

OUR DAILY LIVES ARE BECOMING INCREASINGLY FRAGMENTED. WE are constantly on the move, flitting like gadflies from place to place. We cannot concentrate on one task for more than a few moments before we are forced to move on to the next. Our attention span is growing ever shorter. According to psychologists, the 'now' we recognize is a speck of time lasting approximately twelve seconds. The more continuous or connected these spells become, the greater our feeling of security and repose. It is as if our lives were moving pictures, made up of a series of separate frames. They make sense only when they are linked in sequence and viewed as a whole, rather than as a jumbled collection of disjointed images.

In the modern marketplace we suffer from the disorientating rate of change. Commercial pressures, and the full weight of a highly sophisticated advertising industry, urge us to throw off the old and embrace the new. Whatever we had yesterday must never satisfy us today. Last week's car is judged too slow, last year's kitchen units the wrong design or colour. This restless dissatisfaction is rarely found in gardeners and still less often in pastoral societies. Dorothy Lee, a Harvard University research anthropologist, has made a special study of the people of the Trobriand Islands, and finds that while we in the West are avid for change, they prefer the comfort and security of the tried and tested. The Trobriander 'expects and wants next year to be the same as this year and the year before', she writes in *Freedom and Culture*. They cannot make sense of Western-style advertising, because for them 'the new is not good and the old is known and valued'.

Most of us would find it impossible to avoid the commercial world completely, but at least in our gardens we can embrace the substance and sanity of the real world, where the stimulus of constant change is combined with the reassurance of permanence and constancy. We spend most of our lives in a land of make-believe, where semblance is more important than substance. This is the world of virtual reality, laser images, cyber pets and science fiction, where values are measured in monetary terms and an old master painting can be sold for millions one minute and be valueless shortly afterwards when proved to be a fake. There is no such deception in a garden, where pinks and peas are what they are and cannot pretend to be otherwise. A shrub is either alive or dead. When we plant bulbs we get daffodils and crocuses, not roses and carnations. An overblown rose is an overblown rose, and its appearance cannot be altered by image consultants or spin doctors. Here we work with the genuine and discover what is permanent and true.

When I wrote the provisional notes for this chapter I was sitting in my study on a fine morning at the very onset of spring. The window was wide open and I could watch a blackbird building a nest in the ancient yew tree which borders the north wing of the house. The bird was creating a home for its young, just as its ancestors have done for countless years. In front of me lay the river Severn, in full spate, rolling on its majestic way from the Welsh hills to the Bristol Channel as it has been doing for millennia. The tide had come up at the beckoning of the moon, a journey it has made twice a day since time began. We were approaching the spring equinox and would soon be witnessing some impressive tidal bores, whose heights and times can be anticipated with remarkable precision. In the distance lay the Cotswold hills, now green with the fresh foliage of spring, where Roman troops had fought the Celts and Neolithic man had raised his monoliths and built his burial mounds. Each day the contours of those hills appear to change, seeming flattened at first in the full morning light and then deepening as the shadows fall. My morning paper that day had brought me reports of a turbulent world riven by chaos, but my eyes surveyed a scene of total serenity. The world observed from my study window – looking across the garden to the surrounding countryside – was essentially one of constancy and calm.

At present we are deeply concerned about environmental issues. We are trying to find new sources of energy to replace fossil fuels and more efficient catalytic converters to reduce the toxicity of car exhaust fumes. What a difference it would make if, instead of seeking technological solutions to our problems, we looked for a change in philosophical outlook. At present we assume that we are part of a linear, expanding economy, where there is an inexorable trend towards greater and greater productivity, more and more consumption and ever-growing waste. Our environmental problems would be eased if we reverted to the primeval conception of life as a ceaseless cycle of ebb and flow; if we adopted an ethos in which we produce only what we truly need and where we recycle our waste so that we can use it over and over again. Pollution would be reduced in a culture where we took our pleasures at home rather than in distant Meccas of entertainment; where we produced more of our own food and imported less from abroad; where we spent less time creating fresh wealth, and far more time enjoying the wealth we already possess. Such changes can begin within a Soul Garden, where we can relearn the art of relaxed natural living. Stress arises when we are subject to too much change. This never happens in a garden, where nothing occurs precipitately. The progression from autumn to winter is slow. Day doesn't give way to night immediately; there is always a period of adjustment as the sun's rays weaken and the dusk deepens. The same applies to the major changes in our personal lives – adolescence, the menopause, the ageing process – which are all spread over a period of time so we have a chance to make the necessary mental and physiological adaptations.

In a garden nothing can be hurried. There is a time and place for everything. Each day is a new beginning and every season brings a fresh set of circumstances. Within this therapeutic milieu we learn both patience and hope. If corn can grow in the ruins of a bomb-damaged church, then new life can spring from the wreckage of our human lives. As long as fresh shoots can sprout from the bole of a pollarded tree then there must surely be hope for human renewal. After the desolation of winter comes the rebirth of spring, and few things are more reassuring to a gardener than the enduring cycle of the seasons.

There are certain lessons which can be learned more easily in a garden than anywhere else. It is here that we discover the essential laws of nature. Our private lives may sometimes go through periods of stagnation when everything seems pointless and disjointed, but the moment we enter a luxuriant garden we are reminded that life is characterized by purpose, harmony and growth. The Soul Garden is designed to highlight this cosmic order, by placing emphasis on the constant cycle of death and rebirth and the endless, rhythmical changing of the seasons. This can be stressed by colour-marking the seasons: perhaps by displaying a predominance of yellow aconites, daffodils, laburnum and forsythia in the spring, switching to a white canvas of roses, lilies and clematis in the summer and then moving on to a vibrant, ever-changing colour show of vines and maples in the autumn.

When developed in this way, gardens act as cultural centres just as museums and art galleries do. They become places for growing people as well as plants. A garden is uniquely ours, not because we own the title to the land, but because it gives us a rare opportunity to express our individuality. Moreover, as we interact more closely with nature we find subtle but important changes occur in our attitude and behaviour towards others. We become calmer, more tolerant and more patient.

237

CHAPTER ELEVEN

A Haven of Rest

'Solitude in the presence of natural beauty and grandeur is the cradle of thoughts and aspirations which are not only good for the individual, but which society could ill do without.'

JOHN STUART MILL, *PRINCIPLES OF POLITICAL ECONOMY* (1848)

*J*F THEY ARE TO HAVE A RESTORATIVE EFFECT, GARDENS MUST be havens of rest as well as places of toil. Many people today are working themselves to death. We are so busy making a good living that we have no time to make a good life, and as a result we fall prone to stress-related illnesses such as coronary disease, high blood pressure and peptic ulcers. We fondly believe that work is the solution to all our problems. If we need more money, extra power or greater success all we have to do, we imagine, is work a little harder. This belief arose during the Industrial Revolution, when production was labour intensive and growth could be achieved only by hard manual toil. These conditions no longer prevail. We live in an age of automation when machines should be carrying out the routine tasks, leaving us free to enjoy a wealth of increased leisure time. Nowadays we should be working smart, not hard.

Many people in the Third World lack the support of labour-saving equipment, and yet their lifestyles are invariably more relaxed than ours. A Kung Bushman of the Kalahari Desert works for about fifteen hours a week, most of which is spent hunting and fishing, pastimes which many of his macho Western counterparts would love to pursue if only they had the time and money. We pay to go on expensive holidays in the South Sea Islands, where we bask in the sun and do those delightfully lazy things that the native islanders do every day of their lives. Is this progress?

During the eighteenth century the cities and towns of Europe were becoming increasingly crowded, dirty and noisy, so gardens were created to provide oases of peace and quiet. According to a contemporary French hygienist, René-Louis

Girardin, gardens should be constructed to be 'tranquil and solitary so that nothing distracts the soul'. That should be our aim today, to design gardens which are an invitation to tranquillity and repose. At present we work harder and harder to produce more and more services and goods, which other people can afford only if they too are prepared to step up their work output. Since there is a limit to the amount we can actually consume we have to create artificial wants. We swallow the blandishments of the advertising industry and assume that we truly *must* have a more powerful computer, holiday home, digital camera, extra car or wide-screen television.

At some point we need to question this scale of values. Do we live to work, or work to live? Do we prefer longer working hours and more money, or more leisure time to spend at home with our family and friends? Men and women have existed on this planet for a million and a half years, and it is only in the last two centuries that we have become industrial animals, caught up in the frantic desire for material possessions and economic growth. Before that time the peasants worked just hard enough to satisfy their material needs. Today only 6 per cent of the population of the developed countries is engaged in building houses and producing food. So what are the remainder doing? Are the widgets and gizmos we produce really necessary for our survival?

It would be impossible for most people to return to a completely pastoral way of life, but there is little doubt that we would all benefit if we could take a gentle step in that direction. Once again the compromise solution was market tested by Thoreau, who claimed in his diary that he had reduced his demands in order to support himself by working 'perhaps a single month, spring and fall each – so that I must have had more leisure than any of my brethren'. One function of the Soul Garden is to take us away from the economic rat race and expose us to a more natural and restful way of life.

TIME TO SPARE

A SHORT WHILE AGO IT WAS FASHIONABLE TO TALK ABOUT THE 'problem of leisure'. Sociologists warned that we were ill prepared to cope with the vast expansion of leisure time that was bound to be thrust upon us. With the hours hanging idly on our hands we were likely to become increasingly depressed and bored. That doomsday scenario hasn't arisen, except in the lives of the long-term unemployed. The affluent today can no longer be described as the leisure class, since they seem to be working harder now than ever before. Not for them the leisure that even the humblest peasants enjoyed in sixteenth-century England, when the calendar of saints' day and sabbaths provided a total of over two hundred holidays a year. During the week we schedule our leisure time as strictly as we organize our work. On Mondays and Thursdays we aim to go to the gym. On Wednesdays we attend a pottery class at the local college and on Saturdays, if other commitments permit, we try to squeeze in a round of golf. This makes our spare time every bit as pressurized as our working week. We have leisure but no opportunity for idleness; free time, stripped of freedom. Even our weekends are filled with chores. When Saturday comes we escape from business, but not from our constant busyness. Instead of taking a well-earned breather, we clean the car, do the supermarket shopping, chauffeur the children and perform an endless schedule of DIY tasks. Even our play activities are turned into hard graft. We 'work' at our golf swing, compete on the tennis court, and exercise in the gym to the point of exhaustion.

Within our homes, we have dispensed with servants and installed in their place a mass of labour-saving machinery which, in many cases, seems to us busier than ever before. Homes have become larger and better equipped, which means there are more rooms to dust and clean. Moreover, now that most families have a car, few tradespeople provide a door-to-door delivery service. As a result, modern household managers are estimated to spend six times as long on the road, and in shops, as their counterparts did in 1920.

While we are at home or in the office we feel a compulsion to work; in a garden we should feel free to relax. Here we can pioneer a change of lifestyle and working ethos, replacing the Protestant work ethic with a 'satisfaction ethic'. Whenever we are not engaged in absolutely vital work we should take a breather. Even a few minutes' stroll in a garden can have a remarkable calming effect. The story is told of the monk of Hildesheim who found it difficult to understand how a thousand years in God's sight could seem like the passage of a single day. Eventually he left his contemplative studies and wandered into a nearby copse of trees, where for three minutes he listened to the singing of a bird. At the end of this spell of rapt attention he felt that three hundred years had flown. Time stands still and pressures plummet when we take a break in a Soul Garden and allow our minds to withdraw into the state that the poet Andrew Marvell so aptly described as 'a green thought in a green shade'.

In a garden we can be spontaneous, and work as the fancy takes us. One rule of Soul Gardening is 'Never be so busy *working* in a garden that you do not have time to *enjoy* the garden.' Never adhere to a strict timetable of activities but treat the garden as unscripted space, leaving ample time for idle reflection and spur-of-the-moment pleasures. Don't be enslaved by your garden. During our leisure hours we should be free, and not tied to the spade any more than we should be fettered to the computer or the kitchen sink. In Victorian England there was a great upsurge of interest in gardening, but it was gardening as productive work rather than gardening as a source of rest and recreation. This was made clear in the editorial to the first issue of *Amateur Gardening*, published on 2 May 1884, which said: 'This paper is not for idlers of any class; we forbid them to read it!' Within a Soul Garden we need to strike the right balance between work and rest. We should never feel guilty about taking our ease, basking in the sun and sipping a refreshing drink. These moments are more precious now than ever before because of their increasing rarity. This is in keeping with the economists' theory of diminishing marginal utility, which states that the less you have of any particular commodity – whether coffee beans or leisure time – the more valuable it becomes.

EASY DOES IT

GARDENS MUST BE EASY TO MAINTAIN, IF THEY ARE TO SERVE THEIR function as places of rest and recreation. Before the Second World War the great gardens of England gave employment to retinues of servants. More than sixty full-time gardeners worked in the grounds of Exbury, one of the Rothschild family's smaller English mansions. Those days are gone. Few people today can afford a full-time gardener, so we must all become self-reliant. This is one of the great dilemmas of Soul Gardening, for it is when we are too busy to maintain a garden that we most need the peace and sanctuary that a garden can provide.

There is no doubt that the physical exertion of gardening is beneficial for both body and soul. Regular digging, hoeing and weeding provides a valuable source of aerobic exercise which helps to promote the efficiency of the arteries, lungs and heart. Using a technique known as Doppler imaging, a team of scientists from the University Hospital in Freiberg, Germany, examined fifty healthy men and found that those who gardened for a minimum of two afternoons a week improved the elasticity of their artery walls. The regular bending and stooping serves to maintain the strength and suppleness of the trunk and legs, and the energy employed helps to combat the build-up of unwanted fat. We benefit from this gentle workout, but also gain enormously from the rest and relaxation which a garden can provide. To strike the ideal balance between these two opposing activities – work and rest – is never easy and depends entirely on one's personal situation. If you have little time to spare, it's obviously foolish to attempt to maintain a labour-intensive garden. On the other hand, if you're retired or temporarily unemployed, you may welcome the chance to spend a large part of your day in your garden, growing prize vegetables and flowers. If you have a high-pressure job, you need a garden in which you can relax rather than work. In these circumstances your first investment might be a good reclining chair rather than a greenhouse or a mechanical rotavator.

One of my overworked patients told me, 'A garden is a thing of beauty and a chore for ever.' If you are in that frame of mind and find gardening more of a bane than a boon, I strongly urge you to review your current gardening tasks. Make a list of all the irksome chores and then decide how best they can be eliminated or reduced. If you are tired of weeding the patio, have it relaid on a polythene liner to check the growth of weeks. If you have a box hedge which needs constant trimming, consider replacing it with a low stone wall. Put a mulch around the rose trees to keep out all but the most vigorous weeds. Fill in bare earth with ground-cover plants. Exchange weed-filled beds for patios and crazy-paved terraces, softened by patches of evergreen shrubs and rockery plants.

Anyone can work hard; the secret of successful Soul Gardening is to work easy. This can be done by joining one of the oldest of all ecological movements, the no-digging method of gardening, described in Chapter 2. We risk damaging the delicate root network of flowers and shrubs whenever we disturb the soil with a spade or hoe. If depth digging is needed to aerate the ground, leave the job to the earthworms. Large weeds can be pulled by hand and the rest smothered with a good layer of organic compost. Women generally have a far more caring approach to gardening than men, who are rarely happier than when they are dominating their environment, felling trees, ripping up weeds and excavating the soil. Anthropologists find an explanation for this obsession in ancient mythology, where the warm, fertile earth is generally portrayed as the female principle, and the spade or plough as the symbol of male potency. According to this exegesis, men commit a symbolic rape of mother earth every time they thrust a spade into the ground. This is still the belief of Native Americans, many of whom do not plough the ground because they feel it is equivalent to taking a knife to rip their mother's flesh.

A second aid to easy gardening is to take full advantage of indigenous plants which need the minimum possible care and attention. In eighteenth-century England it was fashionable to acquire and cultivate exotic flowers, shrubs and trees imported from around the world. That was when the plantsman's troubles started. Flowers were introduced – orchids, fuchsias and pelargoniums – which fared well in their native lands but struggled to survive in the English climate. Growing hothouse flowers can be a fascinating and rewarding hobby, but if time is short it is far better to select hardy, native plants. The *feng shui* garden experts claim that it's bad luck to have sickly plants in a garden because it kills *chi*, the life force. To my mind they should be banned because they create an ambience of weakness and decay, whereas a Soul Garden should be an expression of rampant, burgeoning life.

Once the exotica arrived, horticulturists experimented with various methods to keep them alive. Techniques were developed to make it possible to grow rhododendrons and camellias in alkaline soil, by treating the earth with regular dressings of sulphur, garden compost, peat and ammonium sulphate. But the results are often disappointing. One experienced gardener carried out these measures assiduously for twenty-five years and managed to achieve only a marginal reduction in the alkalinity of his soil (a drop in pH from 8 to 7.9, still on the alkaline side of the neutral point of pH 7). We must each decide if we want to sustain this effort. Should we struggle to fill a garden with azaleas, in adverse soil conditions where they are constantly prone to chlorosis and defloration, when the land could be stocked with hardy hollies and laurels? Using peat-filled containers might suit some gardeners, but growing camellias in pots and feeding them with weekly doses of ericaceous plant food seems to me like keeping canaries in cages and feeding them with daily doses of bird seed. Far better, in my opinion, to grow indigenous plants and have nature working as an ally rather than in constant opposition.

The gardening workload can also be eased by planting perennials rather than annuals, and by picking hardy plants and shrubs rather than delicate specimens which need to be wrapped up in the winter or brought indoors to escape the frost. And take careful thought before you create a herbaceous border. These pretty features may be a popular feature of gardening manuals, but they do require an enormous amount of work, including regular weeding, dividing, replacing, tying up, pinning down, staking, dead-heading and thinning out. This is fine if you have time to spare, but not if your moments of leisure are in desperately short supply.

The wilder the garden the better it will serve its therapeutic function. The less you curb, control and cosset it, the more it will flourish. A two-year trial carried out by the Consumers' Association at their demonstration gardens in North London, intended to test the effectiveness of labour-intensive gardening, revealed that many plants fared as well, if not better, when left to their own devices. The lavenders, in particular, produced much better displays of flowers when they were starved of artificial nourishment. Other plants which fared well when unpampered were broom, gorse, buddleia, ceanothus, rosemary, cosmos, clarkia and Californian poppies. 'If you never feed or water a garden you will save a lot of time and effort,' was the report's simple conclusion.

Another attraction of wilderness gardens is that they support a broad spectrum of wildlife. Ninety per cent of British butterflies need local foods on which to lay their eggs. If a garden is without holly there will be no holly blue butterflies. Without honeysuckle there will be a dearth of white admirals, and without buckthorn no brimstones. Without indigenous plants we cannot encourage indigenous wildlife. A horse chestnut tree will support more than a hundred insect species when it is growing in its natural habitat in Spain; in Britain it rarely harbours more than three. Our aim should be to create gardens which appear to have been untouched by human hands and which can be maintained with minimal physical effort.

The wise gardener will also make full use of labour-saving equipment. Never do a job yourself if there is a machine which can do it equally well, unless the task gives you intrinsic pleasure. Why clear a large lawn of debris with a rake when you can do the job so much more easily with an electrically powered scarifier? It would take me several hours to cut my lawn with a hand-propelled mower, whereas I can complete the job in minutes with a tractor mower. This gives me time to sit down, relax and enjoy the result of my labours.

A further aid to trouble-free gardening is to free oneself of unrealistic targets. Let the garden evolve at its own pace, and in a fashion which gives you pleasure rather than frustration and constant disappointment. Never expect to create a *perfect* garden. That would be totally bogus, for nature is never perfect.

The absolutely weed-free lawn is a millionaire's toy: if you really want to see a flawless green carpet, free of daisies and moss, plant Astroturf. We can't expect perfection in a garden, any more than we can expect it in our personal lives. Both Jews and Muslims make a practice of building imperfections into their synagogues and mosques. An odd brick may be omitted, or a token patch of wood left unpainted, to serve as a reminder that the work of man is always flawed. Perfection is to be found only in the work of God.

Some years ago a study was carried out which showed that people with a tendency to migraine were often perfectionists who rarely achieved 'resting points of contentment' in their work. This perfectionism detracts from the benefits of Soul Gardening. Some people are forever tinkering with their gardens, changing this and altering that in the hope that they will eventually achieve the ideal layout. These perfection seekers construct garden paths along which they never have time to stroll, and install garden seats on which they never have a chance to sit. They are like motoring enthusiasts whose cars are always stripped down in the garage. To get the full benefit of a garden, we would do well to remember the words of the *Tao Te Ching*: 'When your work is done, then withdraw! Such is Heaven's Way.'

SOFT FASCINATION

IN A GARDEN THERE IS A TIME TO WORK AND A TIME TO REST. THIS is the natural rhythm of life, which always follows an alternating cycle of activity and repose. Trees and shrubs are active during the spring and summer but take a long, recuperative break during the winter. Our hearts are in non-stop action from the time we are born to the moment we die. They are able to keep up this ceaseless pumping because they follow a strict work–rest cycle. After each short contraction (systole), the heart takes a longer pause (diastole) to recover from its exertions. Babies follow a similar routine when they suck at their mother's breast, drawing on the nipple for bursts of roughly ten seconds and then resting for a slightly longer time. This activity–rest cycle represents the biological rhythm which most animals follow. Ants are thought to be constantly at work, and yet they have been found to rest 80 per cent of their time. Bees are judged to be equally busy creatures, and yet they spend 50 per cent of their time resting. Even the industrious beaver leaves its lodge for only about five hours a day. We work a far longer day, largely because we are the only species that spends a large part of its time engaged in activities which are not essential for its survival. In an ideal world we would follow the example of the animal kingdom and spend much of our day in rest. Tests in factories show that the introduction of a five-minute rest pause at the end of every working hour leads to a lessening of tiredness and an increase in production of roughly 13 per cent. This is the pattern we should follow in a Soul Garden, where we should work in short stints rather than for protracted periods. If we work in this way we will also increase our exposure to the *vis medicatrix naturae* or healing powers of nature.

When we devote our attention to simple tasks such as planting bulbs or pruning roses we forget our everyday cares and woes. Our brains are active but untroubled, so that we are in the relaxed state of mind which horticultural therapists describe as 'soft fascination'. As Frederick Law Olmsted, the designer of Central Park, said in 1865, 'Nature employs the mind without fatigue and yet exercises it; tranquillizes it and enlivens it.' When we are in this relaxed mood, in close touch with nature and far removed from everyday worries, we are free to devote our minds to meditation, as the Cistercian monks did when they were each given their own plot of land within the walled gardens of their monasteries. Tending these small gardens formed a part of their daily spiritual discipline, for they lived by the maxim *Laborare est orare*, to work is to pray.

When we are overtired, as we may be on long driving trips, our eyes close for a few seconds so that we can snatch what has come to be known as 'micro-sleep'. By the same token we need the refreshment of brief spells of 'micro-rest'. Somehow we must reduce the incessant pressure of our working lives. If hospitals can be built with therapeutic gardens, so too can new office blocks. A morning break should involve far more than a quick dash to the coffee machine. Instead it should provide a spell of micro-rest, when for a few seconds we can take time out to gaze at a tank of tropical fish, water the window box or tend the plants in the office terrarium. During the lunch hour it should be possible to stroll round a neighbourhood park. Even a few moments looking out of the window can have a calming effect, for tests carried out by Rachel and Steven Kaplan of the University of Michigan have shown that employees experience fewer headaches, less stress and greater job satisfaction when they are working in natural surroundings rather than in the midst of a leafless concrete jungle.

FUN AND GAMES

WORK NEEDS TO EMBRACE THE ELEMENT OF PLAY. LIKE HENRY Ford, we should be able to say at the end of our careers, 'I never did a day's work in my life – it was all fun.'

Most animals have a well-developed sense of fun. Cats juggle with balls of wool, dogs chase after sticks, elephants play practical jokes with buckets of water and whales give their calves piggyback rides and shower them with bubbles of air. We, by comparison, seem remarkably staid. By the time we reach adulthood we have frequently crowded our lives to such an extent that we are too busy for spontaneous fun and games. Yet whenever we describe our ideas of paradise, we invariably think of it as a place of pleasure and play. When the Greeks pictured the Isles of the Blessed they viewed them as a work-free haven where the inhabitants spent their time riding, playing draughts, making music and taking part in strenuous games. The Celts had a similar vision of their Shining Land, a place where people feasted, sang, played music, made love, raced boats and chariots and competed in vigorous sports.

In an ideal world there can be little doubt that we should find more time for fun. The Hindus believe that the world was created for this very purpose, so that we would be free to indulge in *lila*, or 'play'. Philosophers believe that it is through play that we expand our personalities. 'As soon as a man apprehends himself as free and wishes to use his freedom,' wrote Sartre, 'then his activity is play.' Sociobiologists such as E.O. Wilson have pointed to the importance of communal games as a way of encouraging co-operative social behaviour, and many of the great educators have suggested that play should form the cornerstone of childhood training. Friedrich Froebel evolved a new system of education based on instructive play, which he regarded as 'the most spiritual activity' for youngsters. His concept of the ideal nursery school was a garden where children could learn through active play – hence the term *kindergarten*, which formed the title of one of his earliest books. This outdoor classroom was equally important for adults, claimed Froebel, as it provided 'joy, freedom, contentment, inner and outer rest, peace within the world'.

As we have seen, many of the early gardens were designed to meet this need for active play. In Tudor England the leisure gardens of the aristocracy provided opportunities for bowls, hawking, archery, tennis and croquet. Many years later public parks were established, equipped with tennis courts, putting greens, boating lakes and bowling lawns, to satisfy the recreational needs of the working classes.

Today few private gardens provide facilities for sport, even though many of us could find room to introduce croquet, boules, badminton, quoits, volley ball or skittles – games which can be enjoyed by family and friends alike. Instead of creating traffic jams and pollution by driving our children to theme parks and swimming pools, we could entertain them *en famille*. Just think of the benefits which would result if we spent, say, 10 per cent of our leisure time in our own gardens.

NATURAL SEDATION

NOW MORE THAN EVER WE NEED THE PEACE WHICH GARDENS CAN provide. When we stay indoors we are tempted to read the papers and watch the news on TV. The media give us an impression of a world full of violence, strife and greed, but the moment we step into a garden we enter an entirely different world, one which is non-threatening, harmonious and serene. Instead of being bombarded with images of death and destruction, we are surrounded by evidence of natural life and growth. Here we find the comfort and hope to replace our existential angst. One of my great pleasures when I visit New York City is to relax for a while in the courtyard garden of the Frick Museum, which offers an oasis of peace and serenity in what must surely be the busiest metropolis in the world. The keynote of this garden is simplicity. It was designed by Russell Grant, who avoided all attempts at creating dramatic effects on the grounds that 'even a mild shock of surprise is opposed to the idea of tranquillity which I consider more than ever essential in a city garden'. In a peaceful setting like this we cease to be aware of the relentless ticking of the clock and become more conscious of the eternal present.

In a tranquil garden we leave behind our ugly moods and damaging emotions. Here we can begin to relax and let nature soothe away our stress; we can find strength in repose, by drawing on the energy which surges from every twig and blade of grass. To absorb that power, imagine yourself to be a tree. Stand with your feet firmly planted on the ground and picture your roots sinking deeply into the soil from which they are drawing a steady stream of nourishment. Then raise your face and arms towards the sky so that you can absorb the energy coming from the sun. Breathe deeply and think of the energy which is flowing into your body from the earth, air and sky. Imagine yourself to be part of the cosmic whole, drawing strength without effort from the universal life force. Take time to experience the peace. Absorb it into your being. Still your body and your mind, set aside the worldly din, go deeper into the silence and listen to the still voice of nature. Then, as you re-enter the world of rush and bustle, carry with you the peace that your garden has brought.

sanctum s

The ideal garden symbolizes the marriage between time and eternity. It is a place in which we work, in order to derive more enjoyment from our leisure time. The busier we are, the more precious those moments of rest and relaxation become. The gentle physical action of weeding and pruning can be the perfect antidote to stress, but the gardening workload must never become so onerous that we have no time to rest and enjoy the fruits of our labours. The burden can be eased in numerous ways. We can develop a more tolerant attitude to weeds, which have a beauty of their own and are in any case only displaced plants. Bare patches can be filled with ground-cover plants, for bare earth is the vacuum which nature abhors. Ground-cover roses are excellent for this purpose, especially varieties such as 'Flower Carpet' and 'Bird' which do not sucker, do not need dead-heading, and can be pruned with a hedge trimmer.

The Soul Garden is a place for 're-creation', a process of physical restoration which is best achieved when a balance is struck between horticultural work, rest and play. When this equilibrium is attained the garden becomes what the Romans described as a sanctum sanctorum, a place of sacred retreat, privacy and peace.

CHAPTER TWELVE

Common Ground

'So when your work is finished, you can
wash your hands and pray
For the Glory of the Garden, that it
may not pass away.'

RUDYARD KIPLING

*T*HIS BOOK WOULD BE INCOMPLETE WITHOUT THIS FINAL chapter, for a study of the therapeutic, holistic approach to gardening must include its social role. According to the existentialist philosophers, our relationship to the world can be considered under three main headings, the *Eigenwelt*, *Mitwelt* and *Umwelt*. The first category, the *Eigenwelt*, is the inner world of the self, which we have explored in the earlier chapters of the book describing the ways in which gardens can be used to further personal discovery, fulfilment and growth. The third category, the *Umwelt*, refers to our relationship with the universe. This field has also been discussed in earlier chapters, which have emphasized the benefits which can be gained by forging closer links with the natural world. This leaves for consideration only the second category and third leg of the existential stool, the *Mitwelt*, which relates to our relationship with other people. This is the all-important theme of this final chapter.

Few people will deny that there has been a weakening of community ties in recent years. Now more than ever we live in a social vacuum. Our nomadic lifestyle with its frequent job changes makes it difficult for us to establish strong local roots. Many people lead dormitory existences, commuting long distances to work and returning home late at night only to eat and sleep. To save time and money we buy our food in impersonal supermarkets rather than at the friendly corner shop. We travel by car instead of on foot, which separates us from our neighbours, and we entertain ourselves at home in splendid isolation rather than in the village hall or cinema. As a result we have neighbourhoods without neighbours. This applies particularly to metropolitan areas, where people may live for years without once meeting their next-door neighbour. This social alienation is having an adverse effect on our health, for medical research has shown that lonely people are less able to cope with stress than those who have the support of family and friends. They are also more prone to accidents, mental illness, suicide, cancer, tuberculosis and heart disease.

Nowadays we are encouraged to think of ourselves as part of a global community. But whatever progress is made in communication technology in the future, it will always be difficult for us to feel genuine empathy for a social unit which is so disparate and vast. We can send e-mails to people living on the other side of the world and join discussion groups on the Internet, but this is no substitute for intimate personal contact, seeing, touching and hugging.

In the past communities came together for two main reasons, to celebrate and to make war. The word *celebratio* means 'people together'. Whole communities joined together to observe festivals, holidays, games, feasts, fairs, saints' days, carnivals, circuses, markets, rites and wakes. The more they celebrated these events the more closely they were linked, and the less occasion they had to make war. Many of the revelries had strong pagan roots and made prominent use of natural symbols. The winner of the Roman games was crowned not with gold but with a laurel wreath. The focal point of the early Christmas festivals was not the presents but the holly, mistletoe, yule log and fir tree. Trees were planted to mark coronations and centenaries, palm leaves plaited at the festival of Easter, and pumpkins hollowed for Hallowe'en. Today we still feel an urge to celebrate these ancient folk festivals even though our lives are far removed from our pastoral roots. We do so for social reasons, because we enjoy the feeling of kinship that comes from taking part in public celebrations.

COMMUNAL PLAYGROUNDS

MOST OF THESE FESTIVITIES TOOK PLACE OUT OF DOORS, IN PARKS or open forests, on heaths or village greens. People joined together to light bonfires, dance around maypoles or spit-roast an ox on a frozen lake. For primitive people the communal meeting place was generally a well-marked clearing beside a sacred spring or holy tree. When cities were built this open meeting area became the *agora*, which served as both a market-place and a centre of private and public assembly. At a later stage some of these civic functions were transferred to special-ized buildings: shops, town halls, commercial exchanges and courts of justice. But people still needed to meet and mingle and exchange the gossip of the day, so the *agora* was transformed into a public square, a *plaza* or a *piazza*.

Public gardens and parks were much later social develop-ments. They were created when cities lost their fields and became so densely developed that there were no open spaces left for public gatherings. Vauxhall Gardens in London was a social success from the moment it opened its gates in 1660. It was developed as a commercial venture over a period of four years, to meet the need for a romantic landscape garden where people of culture could gather to share their entertainment. Covering an area of twelve acres, the gardens offered lantern-lit walk-ways, supper boxes painted by Hogarth and hedged arbours where lovers could meet for secret assignations. In the centre a grand concert hall provided the venue for plays and musical events. On one occasion a crowd of over twelve thousand people caused a three-hour jam of carriages on Westminster Bridge as they made their way to Vauxhall to enjoy a performance of Handel's 'Music for the Royal Fireworks'. Other public gardens, among them Kensington and Ranelagh Gardens, followed shortly afterwards and became the new centres of London social life, attracting many eminent people. Samuel Pepys recorded in his diary the convivial evenings he spent at Vauxhall Gardens, where with great pleasure he 'walked, and ate, and drank, and sang'.

A century later there was a move to convert the paved town squares into neighbourhood gardens, a trend which was promoted by the great landscape designer Humphrey Repton on the grounds that it would improve the beauty of the metropolis and enhance the health of its inhabitants. Later came the creation of public parks, for the enjoyment of the less affluent classes. These were hugely popular and sprang up with amazing speed. Before 1840 there wasn't a single public park in Britain; thirty years later, every major town in Britain had a neighbourhood park where people could congregate for their off-duty fun and games. The first such park was built at Birkenhead, just across the Mersey from the thriving port of Liverpool. Its development was presented as a philanthropic gesture, whereas in fact it was an exceedingly shrewd investment. Its main purpose was to raise the development value of the surrounding land, which wealthy industrialists were willing to buy at a premium in order to live in a mansion with a frontage on a prestigious public park. The same applied to Regent's Park, which was developed by the Crown Commissioners with the sole purpose of boosting the value of the Crown properties which bordered it.

Nowadays many public parks in depressed urban areas have fallen into disrepair and become the haunts of vandals and drug addicts. This dereliction is to be deplored, for city parks are valuable places for rest and relaxation. Surveys conducted in America show that the three most important reasons people cite for visiting city parks and gardens are 'relaxation, stress reduction and inspiration'. People wander into parks to re-establish their links with nature, to admire the trees and feed the birds. Even a crowded city like New York provides a home for 350 different species of bird, a population which is swelled in the spring by more than three hundred migrating species including ospreys, Kentucky warblers and marble godwits. And not only are these parks havens for naturalists; they also serve an important social function. We live today in fragmented, multi-racial communities. If we wish to heal the rifts within these communities and foster a spirit of group identity, we would be well advised to restore our public parks to their previous prominence as places of communal meeting and celebration. Voluntary organizations are set up to support the running of museums and schools, so why not bring together bands of local activists to develop the use of town squares and public parks? What better way could there be to mark the start of a new millennium than to restore our communal parks and gardens to something of their erstwhile glory?

OUTDOOR SPREADS

THESE OPEN SPACES CAN BE MADE THE FORUM FOR A WIDE VARIETY of public entertainment. Anything which encourages people to come together to share their pleasures should be fostered. Events should be varied to meet the needs of both young and old: pop festivals, jazz, classical music, flea markets, plays, puppet shows, competitions, displays, pageants, festivals, races and games. We are so used to finding our entertainment indoors that we tend to forget the delight that comes from traditional outdoor fun which is shared with total strangers rather than with groups of carefully selected friends.

The bonding which takes place on these occasions is particularly strong when it involves the sharing of food. This is the true meaning of company, a word which is thought to derive from the French *comme pain*, 'with bread'. Celebrations in pagan times drew people together because they invariably involved communal feasting, dancing and drinking. Today, when most of our eating is done alone, we lack these bonding experiences. Even the family meal seems to have been replaced by the solitary TV supper.

One way we could strengthen our sense of community is by staging more shared meals. Unlike the majority of primitive races we are not particularly generous with our wealth. We don't hold lavish potlatch ceremonies in which we set out to overwhelm friends and neighbours with our extravagant hospitality, and when guests admire our prized possessions we don't donate them as gifts. Nor do we readily write out cheques, or even offer modest loans, when our friends are in financial trouble. But we do seem prepared to share our food and drink, even if it is only a chocolate biscuit and a cup of tea. This mild tendency towards altruism is something on which we should build if we wish to strengthen our friendships and community ties.

Nowadays social entertaining has become so complex that it has ceased to serve this simple communal function. Providing friends with an elaborate haute cuisine meal is a costly and laborious process. As a result perhaps we give fewer dinner parties than we should. We forget that the quality of the companionship is what matters, not the lavishness of the food. Better a dinner of herbs served with love than a laboured banquet of *filet de boeuf en croûte*.

To reverse this trend we ought to revert to the practice of giving casual garden meals where the fun is more important than the fare. The traditional picnic is certainly long overdue for revival. This was originally an alfresco meal where people agreed to supply different items, one providing the bread rolls and others the cold meats, salads, cheese or fruit. This shared the burden of preparing a spread for a large group of people, and explains the derivation of the word picnic which stems from the Italian *piccola nicchia*, a 'small task'. The picnic became a cult among the Victorians, and was frequently mentioned in the novels of Dickens, Trollope and Jerome K. Jerome. The Arcadian movement was at its height, and people were inspired by Romantic paintings of scantily dressed nymphs and shepherds eating and drinking in flower-strewn meadows.

In America in the 1930s it became fashionable for people of note to escape from the cities to picnic outdoors in areas of outstanding scenic beauty. One remarkable picnic party was held in the Californian desert, where the guest list included Bertrand

Russell, Aldous Huxley, Krishnamurti, Charlie Chaplin, Paulette Goddard, Greta Garbo and Christopher Isherwood. The gathering ended in semi-disaster, when the local sheriff arrived and accused the party of desecrating the Los Angeles river bed. He demanded to know their identities, but assumed they were lying when they supplied him with their true names. Calling them a bunch of no-good tramps, he pointed to the warning notices, gave them a caution and left.

Providing we observe the Countryside Code, there is no reason why we should fall foul of the law if we follow the example of the Hollywood stars of the 1930s and picnic in the countryside. Gardens and parks are meant to be shared, and there is no better way to do so than by organizing outdoor tea parties, barbecues and picnics.

THE SOCIAL VALUE OF ALLOTMENTS

ALLOTMENTS OFFER ANOTHER SPLENDID WAY OF USING GARDENS TO cement community relations, as we saw in Chapter 2. They are popular not only in Britain, for when the recent Russian domination of Poland ended there was a sudden resurgence of interest in allotment holding. More than a million town dwellers took up allotments, and another 1.5 million joined the waiting list. People were prepared to travel to their plots, which were sometimes several miles from their homes, partly to supplement their food supplies but more especially to enjoy the freedom and comradeship of the countryside. Instead of erecting tool sheds, some owners built cabins which they used as weekend retreats. These allotments may have started out as places to grow vegetables, but their real value, according to a Polish sociologist, were as 'sites for social and family gatherings'.

In 1962 the New York Housing Association – the world's biggest landlord – launched a gardening competition for its tenants, in which anyone who wanted to enter was given a plot of cleared ground and a grant to buy seeds, plants and fertilizers. From that moment onwards they were free to develop the allotments as they pleased. Every August the housing sites were visited by a team of horticultural experts who awarded certificates to every plot holder as well as prizes for the gardens which merited special praise. The scheme was relatively cheap to administer and produced gains which were both social and aesthetic. As one participant said, 'From early morning to late at night you can see neighbours leaning over the garden fence. It has become the centre spot of our court where everyone is a friend.'

The social value of allotment holding is no new discovery, for Plato in his *Republic* recommends that in an ideal society everyone should be given two allotments, one close to the city and the other at some distance from its walls. This would ensure a fair distribution of the more valuable land, and double everyone's chances of making friends. Any person today who fancies some healthy outdoor exercise and wants to increase their circle of friends should consider becoming an allotment holder. In the same way, any civic authority which wants to foster the community spirit should follow Plato's advice and set aside land for allotments, rather than for commercially profitable building programmes.

As an alternative, since there are often long waiting lists for allotment plots, it is sometimes possible to 'adopt' a garden.

Retired people, with time to spare, can undertake the care of gardens owned by those who are so committed to their work that they have no time for garden maintenance. A similar deal can be struck by the young who live in flats and bedsits, who may wish to look after gardens owned by elderly or disabled neighbours.

OUTDOOR ENTERTAINMENT

GARDENS SHOULD BE SHARED AS WELL AS USED AS PLACES OF private pleasure. Most of the world's great gardens were originally created as centres of entertainment. When the gregarious Pope Pius IV developed the Vatican gardens, he ordered the building of a large casino where he proceeded to spend much of the day wining, dining and talking with his friends. The Alhambra Gardens were used for lavish fêtes and parties, as were the magnificent gardens of Vaux-le-Vicomte, where France's finance minister Nicholas Fouquet made the fatal mistake of entertaining the young King Louis XIV to a lavish twelve-hour party. This included three sumptuous meals, a ballet performance, a specially commissioned play by Molière put on in an outdoor theatre and a spectacular firework display. The King was so envious of the gardens, which at the time far surpassed those at Versailles, and was so sure that his finance minister must have paid for them by dishonest means, that he clapped Fouquet in gaol and sequestered his assets.

At a more lowly point on the social scale were the vicarage gardens of Victorian and Edwardian England, which were widely used as venues for summer fairs, bring-and-buy sales and afternoon teas. To raise funds to repair the clock tower they might become the setting for a fête, where village children could bowl for a pig or take part in a lucky dip, while their mothers browsed through the second-hand bookstalls and their fathers tried their skill at the coconut shy. These gardens are a fast-disappearing part of the English heritage, for in order to make financial savings the church authorities have sold off many of the large rectories and moved their incumbents into modern houses with minute gardens. One English clergyman who upholds the parish priest's traditional open-house policy at his large rectory in Norfolk explains: 'Our attitude is that the house and garden is property belonging to the parish, and we're just privileged to have it most of the time. We revel in the opportunity for others to come and enjoy it.' There is no better use for a garden than in providing for the entertainment and pleasure of neighbours and friends.

CO-OPERATIVE GARDENS

ONE OF THE MOST EXCITING HORTICULTURAL DEVELOPMENTS IN recent years has been the expansion of community gardens. These have transformed the appearance of many derelict inner-city areas. Disused parking lots, cluttered with litter and overrun with drunks and drug addicts, have been turned into miniature parks filled with flowers and shrubs. Walls previously plastered with graffiti are now festooned with trellises of colourful climbing plants. Tenement window sills which were once obscured by unsightly lines of washing are now decked with window boxes. This movement had its birth in New York

City in the early 1970s, when Liz Christy, a painter living in Greenwich Village, determined to improve the appearance of the Big Apple. With the help of a band of like-minded friends, who were soon dubbed the Green Guerrillas, she set out to plant flowers on traffic islands. Derelict sites were bombarded with 'seed bombs', balloons filled with seeds, soil and water. A further advance was made when a permanent garden was created at the corner of Bowery and Houston Street, a landmark development now known as the Liz Christy Garden.

At this point the city authorities began to take note of the improvements which were being made. An annual grant was allocated to support Operation Green Thumb, a campaign which has led to the creation of 750 community gardens in New York City. These gardens are reversing neighbourhood blight and making the metropolis a more beautiful place in which to live and work. They are also fostering a stronger sense of neighbourliness. In the words of one participant, 'The garden is a great focus for the community. In this city, where everybody lives in their own little apartment and rushes from home to work and back again, it's hard for neighbours to get together.' The more transient the population, the greater the need for these horticultural meeting places.

The development of communal gardens invariably gives rise to an increased feeling of well-being, heightened self-esteem, greater sociability, cleaner streets, revitalized neighbourhoods and less crime and vandalism. A national study in America has shown that 'access to nature' is the strongest predictor of satisfaction among local residents, and second only to a congenial marriage in predicting general contentment. When European cities were expanding at the height of the Industrial Revolution, a determined effort was made to bring the country into the town. This quest was pursued with utopian fervour, so much so that Parisians called their tree-lined central street the Champs-Elysées – the Elysian Fields. William Penn had a similar idea when he founded the state of Pennsylvania, setting out to create Greene Countrie Townes where there would be one wild acre for every ten acres of developed land. He called these visionary settlements 'Cities of Brotherly Love'.

There can be little doubt that people are happier, and feel closer to their neighbours, when they are surrounded by birds, trees, flowers and shrubs. This was clearly demonstrated by the remarkable experience of Bill and Peggy Mann, who bought a run-down sandstone house in a crime-ridden street in West Manhattan. The windows of the house were pitted by bullet holes. The fire hydrant outside marked the boundary between the territories of two youthful gangs, a bunch of black lads called the Young Kings and their Puerto Rican enemies the Spanish Angels. The neighbouring houses were dilapidated and let to prostitutes, drifters, drug addicts and thieves. Police cars patrolled the street by night and eventually a curfew was introduced to make it a no-go area an hour before midnight. Soon after they moved in, a youngster was killed in a gang fight. The Manns were dismayed but not defeated; Bill, born in London, remembered the brightly painted window boxes that were often used to transform the appearance of rows of drab terraced houses and he had an idea.

Postponing the renovation work he had planned to do on his house, Bill turned instead to making window boxes. After buying several hundred dollars' worth of petunias, ivies and geraniums, he enlisted the help of some of the local gang members, and together they gave the boxes a coat of paint, stocked them with plants and then sold them around the neighbourhood for whatever price they would fetch. With the proceeds they bought more plants and troughs, until eventually they had distributed nearly one hundred and fifty window boxes. The area was transformed. And then, as Peggy Mann recalled in her book *The Street of Flower Boxes*, a miracle began: 'Bright new curtains appeared, and torn window shades were replaced. Newly polished doorknobs gleamed. Landlords provided more outdoor rubbish bins . . . Some people from neighbouring streets came to walk down ours, to gaze, to admire. Pride started blooming again along with the flowers.' Slowly the gang war abated.

The metamorphosis was so remarkable that, some years later, the National Broadcasting Company decided to make it the subject of a TV documentary. Another derelict road had to be chosen as the location for the film for by this time the Manns' street was looking far too smart. Actors recreated the story, decorating the street with gaily painted window boxes which were left in place when the shooting ended. Within a few days the same miracle had occurred: new curtains were once again hung to complement the flowers, front doors were cleaned and painted, and a team of neighbours got together to turn an empty building site into an attractive community garden. The producers of the TV documentary were staggered by the magnitude of the change. 'Suddenly there was something new in the air,' they said. 'The block had become a neighbourhood.'

Similar transformations have occurred in England in deprived inner-city areas. When the Reverend Andrew Mawson took over a church in Bromley-by-Bow, in the East End of London, he found a meagre congregation of a dozen elderly women in a church which was capable of seating hundreds. Around the church was a wasteland of dilapidated buildings. 'The only sign of nature for miles was a single plane tree,' he noted. 'I found it very sad.' An improvement had to be made, so he embarked at once on a programme of environmental renewal. He bought a derelict four-acre park from the local council for a peppercorn rent of 99p a year, and donated parts to various sections of the local community irrespective of their faith or ethnic origin. A group of Bengali women decided to use their plot in front of the church to create a Paradise Garden. Other representatives of the local Asian community developed an allotment filled with exotic vegetables. Another volunteer group used their patch to build raised flower beds which could be cared for by people in wheelchairs. The local art group designed a walkway with curved paths lined with ceramic tiles made by local school-children. At first the benches which lined the walk were stolen, so a local artist was commissioned to produce something that would be too heavy to remove except by crane. He came up with two enormous concrete seats in the form of mythical beasts, which delighted the children. At one corner of the garden a new health centre was built with a pond and an eighteenth-century arch reclaimed from a recently demolished local building.

Throughout the development Andrew Mawson insisted that the new buildings should be made to a human scale and with natural materials and graceful, curving forms. 'One of the things I noticed when I first arrived was all the straight lines and boring boxy shapes,' he explained. 'In everything we've done here, we've taken our cue from nature – organic shapes and materials and lots of variety.' The project has restored the life of the local community and is now completely self-supporting. The café, workshop and programme of special events produce an income of £1 million a year. 'It's another lesson from nature,' says Mawson. 'Life flies towards a garden, whether it's birds, butterflies or people – and then it increases, like plants seeding themselves. All we did here was prepare the ground.'

On the other side of the Thames another urban regeneration experiment was conducted, in which gardens were created in front of two troubled housing estates. Professor Alice Coleman of King's College London described the results at the annual meeting of the British Association for the Advancement of Science. Professor Coleman, who has made a detailed study of inner-city violence, told her audience that on the basis of these experiments she could assert that the most effective way of reducing housing-estate crime was to create small, semi-private front gardens under the direct control of each ground-floor household. The introduction of this simple measure on one estate had 'transformed the menacing, anonymous gangs into polite individuals', she said. On another estate 'even racial harassment was reported to have been killed stone dead'. These gardens were created at very little cost, and stand to save thousands of pounds in reduced vandalism, policing, counselling and prison sentences.

Like chameleons we reflect the nature of our surroundings. As President Lyndon Johnson put it, 'Ugliness can demean the people who live among it. What a citizen sees every day is his America. If it is attractive, it adds to the quality of his life, if it is ugly it can demean his existence.' In harsh surroundings we act harshly. In a gentle environment we act with greater kindness and concern. This was demonstrated when the British government persuaded schools to dig up parts of their concrete playgrounds and turn them into gardens. Most of the six hundred schools which took part in the Learning through Landscapes campaign reported a sharp fall in bullying and playground fights. 'Since the landscaping there is no more intimidation and unruly behaviour,' reported one delighted headmistress.

Some city decay is obvious. One can't help noticing the squalor, the poor housing, the overcrowding, the graffiti, the traffic jams, noise and smog. But what really matters is not the visible pollution but the insidious psychosocial deprivation – the pent-up anger, the social alienation, the drabness, the stress, the discontent and lack of beauty. These malevolencies can all be controlled by programmes of urban landscape gardening. All we need are leaders of the calibre of Liz Christy, Andrew Mawson and Bill and Peggy Mann to spark the grand renaissance. In the green cities of the future the façades of shops will be decked with window boxes, hanging baskets will dangle from lamp posts and unsightly hoardings will be replaced by ivy-covered trellises. Traffic islands and roundabouts will be used for sponsored flower displays. Avenues of trees will be planted in leafless streets, and disused parking lots turned into community gardens. Flower sellers will set up their stalls at street corners. The foyers of hotels, offices and shopping malls will become botanical gardens. Prizes will be given for the most beautiful town square and the city street with the best floral decorations.

Even the most densely populated city has space for these improvements, in churchyards and cemeteries, under road arches, on derelict building sites and along the banks of canals and railways. Much of this disused land is in the hands of civic authorities. At present about a fifth of US land is owned by city corporations. If just a fraction of this land could be released for community gardens the urban landscape would be transformed, for there appears to be no shortage of volunteer gardeners keen to undertake the work of amelioration. A 1982 Gallup Poll revealed that over 3 million Americans were then participating in community garden projects, with another 7 million anxious to offer their services the moment a local site became available. The vast majority of the interviewees wanted their neighbourhoods to have a community garden. The demand is strong, the workforce ready. All that remains is for local authorities to take the initiative and release parcels of suitable land. Then the urban greening can begin.

MORPHIC RESONANCE

WE CANNOT REMAIN FOR EVER ON THE SIDELINES, WAITING FOR improvements to be made. So many opportunities have been squandered in the past. Under the Lyndon Johnson administration there were plans to create federal botanical gardens in New York. The project was put on hold because of 'insufficient funding and the country's overwhelming concern with the Vietnam war'. Billions of dollars were available to destroy vast tracts of plants and trees with chemical defoliants and napalm bombing, but not a cent could be squeezed from the national coffers to support a centre of horticultural excellence. The record of other governments is little better. Britain finds cash to promote the elitist arts, but not to fund the regeneration of its inner-city areas. The Royal Opera House alone gets as much annual aid as all the national parks combined, even though it is visited by far fewer people.

But why must we wait for government action? Regeneration can start in our own back yards. Plants and flowers can be made to bloom in our local offices and shops. Something of the splendour of nature can be restored to our neighbourhood streets, gardens and parks. If we do no more than demand action from politicians and civil servants we merely shift the responsibility from 'us' to 'them'. The world is full of voluble eco-warriors; what we want now are eco-workers. Pollution, noise and concrete jungles starved of vegetation are all man-made. We are the culprits, and we are the people best able to remedy our mistakes. We have it within our power to create a greener, more beautiful world. Better by far to plant a single rose bush in a barren garden plot than to complain about the destruction of the Brazilian rainforests. Ecology, like charity, should begin at home.

The aim must be to create a more beautiful world, not in an idealistic never-never land but in the here and now. It is no good dreaming of a bygone Golden Age or yearning for a Shangri-La in some utopian future. Our crusade must be to create a better world today. We must form a bouquet with the flowers within our grasp. Mother Theresa urged her followers to make a constant effort to do 'something beautiful for God'. That something could be the creation of a lovely garden, back yard or window box, a tiny scrap of natural beauty which we can share with neighbours, friends and passers-by. We may be custodians of only a minute fragment of the earth's surface, but if we all agreed to improve the appearance of those tiny patches the overall effect would be immense. Like the development of a patchwork quilt or pointilliste painting, our individual efforts would merge together until we had created first a more beautiful town, then a more beautiful country and finally a more beautiful world. In India there is a saying: 'If all men sweep their door the village will be clean.' This could well be adapted to read: 'If everyone preserved their own gardens, then the environment will be saved.'

Once this greening movement is launched it will rapidly gather momentum, for we are highly imitative creatures. We pick up the moods and mores of those around us. If one person decides to get hooked up to receive satellite television, suddenly the whole district is bristling with dish aerials. This group behaviour is sometimes known as morphic resonance, or more picturesquely as the Hundredth Monkey Phenomenon, a term coined by ethologists after a study had been made of the feeding habits of a colony of wild monkeys on the Japanese island of Koshima. The monkeys were given supplies of raw sweet potatoes which were slightly caked in sand and grit. The dirt made them somewhat unpalatable, until a young female named Imo hit on the bright idea of taking the tubers to the beach and washing them in the sea. During the next few weeks one or two other monkeys followed her example, and then a remarkable change occurred. Suddenly, after a certain number of monkeys had copied Imo, the whole colony began washing their potatoes in the sea. The same phenomenon was observed on neighbouring islands which had no direct contact with Koshima. It seemed that once a critical number of monkeys adopted the habit, an explosive reaction occurred.

The same behaviour is seen in human communities. Here the concept is often known as the 'broken window theory', since it was originally introduced to explain the apparent causal link between trivial acts of vandalism and massive breakdowns of law and order. On numerous occasions social workers have noted that a chain reaction occurs if one window in an apartment block is broken and left unrepaired. After a short while other windows are smashed, which leads to further vandalism. Graffiti appear, litter accumulates and within a short while the whole block becomes a wasteland of squalor and delinquency. Neighbourhoods are not stagnant; either they deteriorate or they improve. Our outlook at present is far too pessimistic. We see the broken window syndrome in operation, but fail to note the transformations brought about by programmes such as Operation Green Thumb. You cannot create beauty by banishing ugliness, any more than you can make peace by abolishing war.

This is one way in which we can meet the demands of the nineteenth-century utilitarian philosophers, who urged us to act in a manner which would ensure that we are advancing the good of all, when we are at the same time satisfying our own personal needs. If we use whatever space we have to create a Soul Garden, we will enhance our own health and happiness, and also advance the welfare of our neighbourhoods. This is both our private joy and our public responsibility, as someone pointed out at the end of the First World War: 'A garden is a public service and having one a public duty. It is man's contribution to the community . . . it is a mark of an upward-looking civilisation that men make beautiful gardens.'

While gardening may not cure all humanity's ills, it does

undoubtedly provide a simple and practical approach to life enrichment. Alfred North Whitehead, one of the more pragmatic of Britain's twentieth-century philosophers, claimed that the main function of human reason was to promote the art of living. Our minds, he said, should be given over permanently to the quest to satisfy the Threefold Urge: to live; to live well; to live better. This book will have served its purpose if it fosters the development of Soul Gardens and promotes the greening of our villages, towns and cities so that we can heal the schism between man and nature and satisfy the Threefold Urge to lead lives of fulfilment, vitality and purpose.

Throughout the ages gardens have served as communal meeting places, open air forums where people talked, played games, entertained their friends and held alfresco family meals. Nowadays much of this social function has been lost. Meals are often not eaten en famille, but in relays around the TV set. We frequently entertain ourselves in relative isolation, either indoors or away from home. Communities are less cohesive because the car has encouraged us to work and play at a distance from our homes, but they could easily be strengthened if we made better use of gardens, both private and communal. Wherever urban gardens have been created there has been a regeneration of inner city areas, a reduction in crime rates and a reinforcement of neighbourhood ties. More still would be achieved if every parish churchyard incorporated a small garden where people could gather for quiet meditation.

One simple way to overcome city blight and environmental despoliation is for everyone to take the responsibility for making their own garden a place of beauty. These small dots of natural splendour would then build up, like the dabs of paint on a pointillist painting, to create a landscape of beautiful villages, towns and countries.

SELECT BIBLIOGRAPHY

Bach, Richard, *Jonathan Livingston Seagull*. HarperCollins, 1994.

Beautiful Gardens of Britain, The. Marshall Cavendish, 1974.

Blueprint for Survival, A. Tom Stacey Ltd, 1972.

Carpenter, Edward, *The Origins of Pagan and Christian Beliefs*. Senate, 1996. (First published as *Pagan and Christian Creeds: Their Origin and Meaning*. George Allen and Unwin, 1920.)

Coats, Peter, *Great Gardens*. Weidenfeld and Nicolson, 1963.

Dubos, René, *Man Adapting*. Yale University Press, New Haven, Connecticut, 1965.

Erikson, E. H., *Childhood and Society*. Hogarth Press, 1964.

Hessayon, Dr D. G., *The Armchair Book of the Garden*. Century, 1983.

Howard, Ebenezer, *Garden Cities of Tomorrow*. London, 1902.

Kellogg, Dr John Harvey, *Why the 'Blues'*. Modern Medicine Publishing Co., Battle Creek, Michigan, 1921.

Laurel, Alice Bay, *Living on the Earth*. Random House, New York, 1971.

Lee, Dorothy, *Freedom and Culture*. Prentice-Hall Inc., 1959.

Prince of Wales and Charles Clov, *Highgrove: Portrait of an Estate*. Chapmans, 1993.

Reich, Charles A., *The Greening of America*. Random House, New York, 1971.

Schama, Simon, *Landscape and Memory*. HarperCollins, 1995.

Shell Gardens Book, The (edited by Peter Hunt). Phoenix House, 1964.

Shewell-Cooper, W. E., *Soil, Humus and Health: An Organic Guide*. Mayflower Books, 1978.

Swinscow, Dougal, *The Mystic Garden*. Hallsgrove Press, 1992.

Trease, Geoffrey, *The Grand Tour*. William Heinemann, 1967.

van Zuylen, Gabrielle, *The Gardens of Russell Page*. Stewart, Tabori & Chang, New York, 1991.